About the Author

Jack Levy was born in 1938. With a Jewish father and C of E mother he was uniquely fortuitous in being allowed the freedom to make his own choice of religious belief. Without the usual 'indoctrinated-faith' bondage, he was able to query the evident inconsistencies and to make informed conclusions. This set a pattern which moulded his entire outlook on life. He started his career as a draughtsman and progressed to Senior Design Engineer. His ability to view situations from an atypical aspect and analyse accordingly gives this book its distinctive, emotive, pertinence.

Dedication

Being of a controversial nature, this book owes its final, much-revised context to all those who have read it through its prolonged progress and made their valuable views known to me. I thank them all, especially Penny Lane Computers' Ed Barrows who has rescued me so often when (as a complete technophobe) I lost control of my moody computer-cum-processor; and Steve Cook from East Anglia Recovery who spent so long trying to find the entire text when it 'crashed'. It wouldn't have reached publication had it not been for my G.P., Dr. Roy Newman of Hempnall's Millgates surgery, whose vigilance in noticing, diagnosing and instigating treatment for prostate cancer, and for the wonderfully caring team at our Norwich Hospital who, hopefully, cured it.

Most of all, this book would be completely different (probably unprintably so) if my treasured wife, Stella, had not spent so many exhausting hours labouring her way through the manuscript each of the many times that it has been revised, and who put me right when my over-enthusiasm might have occasionally got the better of my tact and sensitivity.

Jack Levy

There's None So Blind As He Who WILL Not See

Copyright © Jack Levy

The right of Jack Levy to be identified as author of this work has been asserted by him in accordance with section 77 and 78 of the Copyright, Designs and Patents Act 1988.

All rights reserved. No part of this publication may be reproduced, stored in a retrieval system, or transmitted in any form or by any means, electronic, mechanical, photocopying, recording, or otherwise, without the prior permission of the publishers.

Any person who commits any unauthorized act in relation to this publication may be liable to criminal prosecution and civil claims for damages.

A CIP catalogue record for this title is available from the British Library.

ISBN 978 1 84963 417 5

www.austinmacauley.com

First Published (2014)
Austin Macauley Publishers Ltd.
25 Canada Square
Canary Wharf
London
E14 5LB

Printed and bound in Great Britain

Contents

Important Statement	11
Introduction	13
Foreword	16
Chapter 1	21
An Essential Prologue with an Explanatory Reasoning	
Chapter 2	27
The Urgency and the Current Significance	
Chapter 3	32
If Demand Exceeds Supply, Reform or Perish	
Chapter 4	39
How and Why Certain Statistics are Manipulated	
Chapter 5	45
Collateral Costs and Potential Prudence	
Chapter 6	50
More "Sleight of Hand" Intrigues	
Chapter 7	55
The Object of these Manoeuvres	
Chapter 8	61
Just Why There's "None So Blind…"	
Chapter 9	67
Brass Tacks Time	
Chapter 10	71
Back To Our Origins	

Chapter 11   78
Recognising the Capabilities Evolution has Provided

Chapter 12   81
An Evolved Ability that must first be recognised as such

Chapter 13   85
And There's More…

Chapter 14   91
The Important Sexual Factor

Chapter 15   94
A More In-depth Look at the Psychology that is Involved

Chapter 16   98
It's All a Matter of Self-Control

Chapter 17   102
The Exposure and our Eventual Recognition of Overpopulation

Chapter 18   104
This is Where it Starts to Become Autobiographical

Chapter 19   108
Qualification and Competence

Chapter 20   113
Time for a Little Rationalisation and Validation

Chapter 21   117
Back Down to Earth

Chapter 22   126
So What was all that Waffle About Racing For?

Chapter 23   139
Freedom's Gift of Perception and Discernment

Chapter 24	**142**
Some Logical Conclusions	
Chapter 25	**144**
Sensitive but Essential Observations	
Chapter 26	**148**
Now for Some Really Uncomfortable Reasoning	
Chapter 27	**150**
After the Rationalisation, Some Logical Thinking	
Chapter 28	**152**
Atrocities, Mythology and Sanity Equated	
Chapter 29	**157**
What about the reliability of those ancient records?	
Chapter 30	**163**
Informed Reasoning, or Comforting Fabrications from the Mists of Ancient History?	
Chapter 31	**168**
Time for a Realistic Look at Developments	
Chapter 32	**171**
A Few More Actualities	
Chapter 33	**174**
A Few More Thoughts	
Chapter 34	**178**
Another Aspect	
Chapter 35	**182**
When does Blind Obstinacy become Mindlessness?	
Chapter 36	**185**
We've Prepared the Stage, Now for the Dramatics	

Chapter 37	**190**
More Authenticity	
Chapter 38	**193**
The Choice of which Path to Follow is Ours	
Chapter 39	**195**
Imagine…	
Chapter 40	**199**
Can You See the Similarity?	
Chapter 41	**201**
Every Perspective has its Vanishing-Point	
Chapter 42	**207**
Looking Back in a Different Light	
The Real Facts of Life	**213**
Appendix	**223**

Important Statement

First, this book is unarguably definitive in that it doesn't simply present or elaborate on fundamental topics which we might have been *told* are factual by those who have themselves been thoroughly "processed". In fact, it is distinctive in *impartially* examining the actual origins of certain life-regulating contentions. It puts them into the perspective of new discoveries and evidence so that, in the light of today's knowledge, any conflict with traditional beliefs is fully and logically rationalised. Naturally, it is quite likely that dissension with lifelong understandings could be uncomfortable for some, but even so, common sense demands that rethinking is prudent and logically should be welcomed from an educational aspect. "Definitive", yes, but its acceptance will probably be limited to those who have the honesty and acumen to recognise that we have all been subject to sustained information from our mentors: information that is now increasingly dubious. Hence it is essential that traditional indoctrination is recognised and set aside; neutrality is fundamental if fresh views are to be <u>fairly</u> weighed up. The book's title "There's None so Blind...." applies to those without it. There is another aspect of this writing which needs to be explained; also one which tests traditional standards, and that concerns the basic presentation of certain details. The reason for this is that 'flowery', veiled ambiguities could allow some vital or pivotal points to be misunderstood or misinterpreted by the reader to provide a less uncomfortable or disturbing message. However, bearing in mind the writing's basic purpose, precise understanding has to be paramount. In other words, there's no room for pleasantries where our entire future depends on the perception which demands to be properly registered by the reader, however disconcerting it might be. Further to the above, and also in the interest of clarity, there are some references such as that of comparing our own urges and instincts with those of animals, and some might take offence at these. But why should this be? It is not a great stretch of perception to realise that we *are* just animals, albeit somewhat more advanced. As animals we, no less than all other animals, have been subject to aeons-long imprinting and conditioning. If there's any doubt about that, just look at the strength of the "knowledge" ingrained in our formative years. Such is typical of the level of confrontation that this book employs.

Introduction

We – all seven billion of the human beings who constitute the human race – are in serious trouble. We're blindly stumbling towards a terrible disaster which nobody seems to care about! It's almost as if we are under the naïve impression that, by consciously ignoring it, the pending (*and growing*) cataclysm will somehow just go away. Yet it doesn't take much more than a cursory survey and a minimum of common sense to see that, far from resolving itself, the longer that it's left unrecognised and left to deteriorate, the nearer the situation becomes to being unresolvable. Terminal, in fact, and that's assuming that some method of recovery isn't already beyond our reach.

The problem? It's more of a disaster, and one which will absolutely and inevitably hit us all when the world's uncontrolled and escalating population, in conjunction with its fast-diminishing resources become, quite simply, mathematically untenable. That is unsustainable, non-viable and, as far as human life on Earth is concerned, terminal!

In order to be really accurate, specific and alarming, the first factual problem to be addressed is that of our almost childish inanity in failing to recognise and accept a situation which is right in front of our eyes!

That is what this writing is all about. It tries to realistically make known both the enormity of the impending crisis and the naivety of the apparent "blindness-barrier" that we prefer to hide behind. It's a book that is intended to "bang the drum", to wake us up and out of our self-defeating stupor by highlighting some of the more obvious illustrations as evidence. It is testimony, if you like, which brings into a proper perspective both the magnitude of the approaching calamity and the covert way in which it is being governmentally hidden albeit, as shown, for self-preservation reasons.

The very delicate issue of religion, which is not unconnected with the above and in fact largely responsible for it, is also laid uncomfortably bare. Virtually every doctrine or belief is regarded by its faithful followers as being "above criticism" or it "just mustn't be mentioned." This self-righteousness factor is being made progressively stronger in this way. Then, in the light of such exoneration from debate, any uncomfortably contentious issues which might be raised as a result of frank, logical appraisal are prudently avoided. That prompts another contention: in a democratic world, how can anything on Earth rightly claim immunity from open discussion? It could be, of course, that there is a danger of its being discredited. This arguably invalid and unwarrantable protocol is examined and put into a sensible perspective.

In this writing there is reasoned and methodical rationale, simple observation and applied psychology which leads to logical conclusions, some of which might take issue with traditionally-unquestioned beliefs and understandings that have for so long formed the bases of many different social foundations. Such disparities are put into an open-minded, less pre-conceived frame of reference which, even if discomfiting for some, demands to be assessed in the light of today's scientific and geological discoveries and evidence. After all, isn't that the principle of education?

This manuscript is certainly not an example of light reading, but if you want to have a new look at some serious matters as they really are, rather than from behind the facade by which they are sometimes unwittingly but often exploitatively preached for us to unquestioningly believe, then it's a text that could raise questions. If it ruffles some feathers, surely that factor should not prejudice its authenticity? In fact, for some it may bring into focus some questions that have been just under the surface for a long time. Whatever the situation, the observations, interpretations, rationale and offered conclusions are just that: offered. It is for the reader to balance these against traditional understandings and then, after weighing up the arguments, to draw a personal conclusions about that which is put forward.

Finally, a quotation worth considering: 'It is as fatal as it is cowardly to blink facts because they are not to our taste' (John Tyndall, 1820-1893). The ball is in your court.

Foreword

'Give me the storm and temper of thought and action, rather than the dead calm of ignorance and faith.' (Ingersol, *The Gods*, 1872).

The title of this book says it all: it identifies and puts into a frighteningly obvious perspective the way that mankind is, in effect, walking towards a cliff top with its eyes closed tight in case it sees something nasty! It's the familiar "Ostrich culture", where something which might be difficult to address or even concede is resolved by a naïve, dogmatic rejection! In this case, the penalty for such folly is literally conclusive, and so is mankind's future on this planet of ours!

Exaggerated assumptions? Whimsical speculations? No; just the facts of life as they are, rather than as they have been presented to us by those who, in some cases, have the most to lose by our knowing realities. That's what this book is about: exposure!

It isn't just unsupported scare-mongering.. It is all carefully explained, put into easily-authenticated or identifiable context, and the inferences discreetly offered. Neither is it a highly technical, statistics-and quotations-reliant composition. It is no more, in fact, than an uncomplicated, reasoned and balanced compilation of facts that we can see for ourselves, of historical stories re-viewed through modern eyes, and conclusions that are either credible or even inevitable in the light of today's knowledge.

But therein lies the problem: the immense hurdle that this writing has to overcome.

This is a serious book about serious issues which people prefer to enjoy the comfort of not discussing. Of pretending that it's not there, or that "something'll come along before anything happens". That's how people react to things that they do not like. It happens all the time. However, this isn't fanciful uncertainty, something that might or might not happen. This is reality and it's a crisis that's growing in size the nearer it gets. That is what this book is about.

So, the hurdle? Think for a moment; how do *you* feel about our growing-overpopulation/diminishing-resources conundrum? About the only possible humanitarian solution to it, that is, limiting reproduction? About the fact that the population is doubling every few decades and that our resources are decreasing at a similar rate, and nobody seems to be concerned about it, as if it's of no real importance? That our continuing failure to even acknowledge it is allowing the dilemma to intensify with every day that passes. Are *you* at ease with the *status quo*? Are you certain that *your* kids are going to live in an ideal world? But this is only a part of the compound conundrum. Even more contentiously, this book investigates not only how the unseeing outcome of religious presumption and influences are actually exacerbating this dilemma, it also examines the validity and fundamentals of religious doctrines per se. The pious "infallibility-factor" which most religions enjoy is put under a less-than-intimidated analysis, as are the foundations of the theoretical ideologies that are regularly preached as historical actualities; as *unquestionable* facts rather than as the unsupportable submissions which, simple logic tells us, they really are! So, how easy do *you* feel about a serious investigation into such previously taken-for-granted issues and beliefs, and can you now understand the 'hurdle', or psychological barrier that a book of this nature has to confront? And why the reader's openness and impartiality is absolutely essential if a proper appraisal and conclusion is to be achieved?

Perhaps a little less contentiously, "None so Blind..." associates the symptoms of this sickness with the all-too-evident deterioration in our world's welfare-factor. It looks into failing social stability, general insecurity, financial dependability and so on. It shows how certain cults are able to exploit these weaknesses and global breakdown in order to promote terrorism for their own ends. More locally, the book throws open a few doors to show how some of the more obvious gauges which would reveal our deterioration are manipulated by the government, and made to appear healthy, whilst others are kept well out of sight. All very disturbing.

'Observable facts and feasible interpretations' might describe the pedigree of this book, whilst 'logical outcomes' portrays its strength. It also puts the psychological impacts and biases involved into a clear perspective. These are fundamental issues that are long overdue an airing, but it's done in the nicest possible way.

Other similar writings often depend upon quotations from previous manuscripts or books to validate their conjectures. However, just because a subject has been written or inscribed and can be quoted it does not mean that it is materially correct, or that it has not been exaggerated or embroidered-upon. On the contrary, he who is activated sufficiently motivated to go to the considerable trouble (particularly in the past) to compile such a record, would clearly like, or need, to make it as readably attractive, and, let's say, as interesting as the bounds that his personal conscience might allow him to. He's only human, after all. Also many such records, particularly those that have been around for a long time, are not immune from being altered to suit different politics, so how can they be relied upon?

With only a few non-foundational quotations and no statistics on which its credibility might depend, this text uses only visual evidence, common sense and logical analysis in its ambition to show that which tradition is concealing from us and which is thereby actively preventing our seeking and understanding the actual (as opposed to decreed) facts about our existence here. This brings up the obvious question: does the writer believe in God?

Let's put it this way. The imperative issue is that of evidence, that which is positively confirmable, rather than that of the "But there MUST be..." culture. There is simply no evidence to prove that God doesn't exist, any more than that there is a God. The only 100%-definite is that we, all of us, don't know the answer, and to rule out any research and learning by thinking (and it is merely thinking) that one *does* know, effectively precludes being open to further, and inevitably educational, knowledge. Does that not make sense?

One of my few, but very relevant, quotations is from Søren Kierkegaard (1814-1855): 'There are two ways to be fooled. One is to believe what isn't true, the other is to refuse to believe what is true.'

One of the most cited repudiations against texts of this nature is the argument that certain academics are quite adamant in their beliefs! Equally, though, there are certain intellectuals who are no less adamant in their disbelief. That issue is analysed and, as is explained in some depth, the matter, the sheer unrealised inflexibility and blind strength of early-years formative teachings is put into its proper, rationalised perspective, as is the <u>unrealised</u> danger of its effects.

Finally, there's another question which needs to be answered, and that is "What right or calibre of expertise does this person have to question that which I've happily believed all my life; that which my own parents told me is the truth and which has been confirmed by professionals at school and in our church? Why does he think that his views on life and its foundations should be any more valid than mine? In any case, as things are, any changes in my outlook will only rock the boat socially, so is it not better to leave things as they are?" Three good points, of course, but the first cannot be answered in a few words as, being of such possibly life-changing gravity, it takes an entire section of this book to carefully explain the circumstances which answer it. Indeed, in order to compile a convincing background to how the logic of this contention evolved, it is modestly thought that the biographical section could well provide a welcome and interesting break from the rest of the text. The second point, however, which is similarly analysed, can be briefly put into context with reference to rocking the boat; an honest and candid perusal would reveal that the "boat" is slowly sinking anyway, under the load of its implausibility.

To close, then, this is not a manuscript that may appeal to the light-minded reader, as it studies a lot of often disregarded but very serious matters realistically, rather than masqueraded behind self-protective, complacency-sustaining facades. This is a book that opens up (with full explanations) the virtual

Pandora's Box of the cataclysm ahead of us. – It is not for faint-hearted traditionalists, unless of course they have an underlying suspicion that things might not be quite as cosy and secure as related to the public. Perhaps they are concerned enough about their and their offspring's future to look into this a little further. There's absolutely nothing to be lost by investigation, after all.

Chapter 1

An Essential Prologue with an Explanatory Reasoning

Focusing on beliefs-without-credence and suppositions seen from a fresh aspect

Why? What can be the reason for having such a cautious introduction? The answer: it's because the subject matter of the following composition is uniquely problematic. The contents present a frank disclosure and un-gagging of issues which some readers might feel a little uneasy about. In order that this book isn't flippantly tossed aside as distasteful, it is clearly essential that the writing's subjects and substance provide an interesting and thought-provoking study. Although its lines of reasoning might possibly give the impression of being austere and even confrontational, the evidence that they highlight and the contentions that are subsequently raised are unemotionally realistic and convincingly matter-of-fact enough to ensure the reader's continued perusal.

Put another way, the utterly essential reader-empathy factor has to be very delicately balanced, with the interest component on one side and the discomfort element on the other, in order to achieve its conceptual acceptability. In other words, there might be certain submissions the subjects and analyses of which, at first glance, could be thought too contentious or discomfiting to the reader. It's an automatic impulse to bin anything that is unsettling. On the other hand, if its importance is made obvious and is clearly such that any upset is secondary to the subject matter, its consequences and repercussions, then the book will have achieved its purpose.

Getting this balance right presents an onerous task: that of equating readability against the barrier of dislike, while providing information that people need to know for their own sakes, even if they would rather not know about it. It is a demanding undertaking. It is as a result of this challenge and careful consideration about how best to deal with it that the main elements of this very demanding composition will initially be carefully presented in their ordained sense, with their material consequences, before any investigation about their validity is embarked upon. This care is essential, as there is the paradox of having to introduce situations that are confirmable against beliefs which are both inconsistent and sometimes physically unlikely. All this must be done without offending the reader! Without shirking from stating that which might not be solace to traditional ears, it must be stated that all the observations and contentions will be carefully presented in a clear and unambiguous fashion so that the reader's own logic can be judiciously applied. However, this naturally means that the verbosity and length of sometimes complex rationalisations might be adversely affected. So, for those to whom that which follows is old news, or for those who mightn't need such in-depth explanations, please understand the need for this diligence and bear with it.

Probing into and analysing matters about which some people have very fixed, 'traditional' opinions, i.e. notions which are normally not *expected* to be open to any degree of questioning, it is important at this point to emphasise another issue concerning this article.

Whilst there will be conclusions expressed which are based on geological observations, historical reports, cerebral characteristics, and logical rationale etc., it has to be pointed out that every one of the concepts being offered are presented merely as the writer's personal opinion. However, they are all offered with thorough and appropriate explanations in the hope that, if the reader agrees with that observed and submitted, they might bring into focus new, alternative viewpoints about subjects that for various reasons may have been taken for granted. These are nevertheless perfectly vindicated and hence valid.. We are probably all familiar with matters which we have regarded as beyond question or not to be talked about since childhood. As such, these issues have been considered as being 'above' any normal meaningful and essential authentication. But common sense demands that we ask why.

To be more brutally specific, it is this anomaly that calls into question:

(a) The actuality of certain testimonies which have always been accepted as being factual without any evidence whatsoever to support their unexamined and presumed soundness;

(b) The need, even the simple logic, of unnecessarily and incautiously protracting deep-rooted and considered routines which, if left unaddressed, will be responsible for nothing less than actually endangering human life on Earth. It is crucial, and it is substantiated later in the text.

What are these matters in question? The first is the complex but extremely personal and sensitive one concerning religious beliefs and the fundamental bases which underpin them all. These topics are equated with a few of the ironically unholy activities and randomly-executed atrocities which (directly or indirectly) emanate from or are executed in the cause of religious extremism.

The second issue is, quite simply, one which could result in anything from mass starvation to a revolution, or an instability-created nuclear wipe-out. It is the inane, irresponsible and blind dismissal of the obvious world-wide overpopulation crisis! "But these are personal matters", "sacrosanct and private", "nobody else's business": all these are typical defensive retorts whenever the subject is raised! But are these disdainful repudiations proclaimed so vociferously to avoid the discomfort of having to acknowledge an issue which, at best, is indefensible and unavoidable? To apply some simple logic and to put forward a positive point, if some alternative viewpoints such as those which follow can be thought about in a dispassionate and impartial way and can be quashed with sound and sensible arguments which plainly justify dismissal of the proposed new views then, surely, it must result in these original conjectures being stronger and more substantial for their having withstood openly being questioned. However, whether that is likely can only be assessed after reading and, if not, then that will put their soundness into proper perspective.

Perhaps I can put it another way: if the reader feels that this writing infringes 'personal correctness' in that it ought not call into question matters that have been unconditionally accepted, for whatever reason, throughout one's entire life, or if it should be a case of "this is what I've been told is the 'truth' and, in any case, it's what all the others believe in!"; then, it is argued, with this level of credence, any such proof demands to be substantiated. With such life-directing assertions to have been given unquestioned credence on the strength of nothing more than hearsay or word-of-mouth, without any proper evidence to substantiate them, then is it not basic common sense to pause and have an educated look in an unbiased and impartial manner both at:

(a) The soundness of what you've been told, in particular those assertions that actually rely on un-checkable antiquity for their hardly-credible exploits being acceptable;

(b) The feasibility of other alternatives.

After all, whether or not a theory or a viewpoint succeeds or fails to be verifiable after rational investigation, the result cannot be other than informative, educational and, most important, possibly enlightening knowledge. At the same time, it is clearly to the advancement of one of the two differing factions. As said earlier, what possible harm can a common-sense examination of basic facts do?

That overpopulation and religion are so often defended in such a spontaneous, instinctive and vigorous way surely displays awareness of a fundamental implausibility. That is the strategic necessity for a thorough and in-depth explanatory introduction such as this one. In fact, it is the reality or existence of this almost natural defensive barrier which has to be highlighted, recognised and understood, before either of the defended issues can hope to be put into their proper perspective. Only then can a fair and unprejudiced judgement of the issues' soundness be conducted.

So, if it can be conceded that an open mind is not a sinful one and that, as in any democratic court, both sides of any debate must be heard before a fair and valid decision can be drawn, then the following represents the case for the defence (the side of a contention which the majority dismiss as being in the wrong without, in most instances, even being heard!) So, with your consent, a new look at the evidence.

The defence opens with advice that every observation and subsequent interpretation which might be described in this composition is nothing more than a simple, logical, reasoned analysis that is being offered, as opposed to ordained, to the reader. Second, these submissions are spelt out in uncomplicated, non-statistical, easily-verifiable form, wide-open to being discredited and rejected, which, it's humbly suggested, is more than can be said about the tales we are force-fed from childhood by those who have already been indoctrinated!

A long-winded introduction, maybe, but I hope it clarifies both the reasons for the writing's possibly prolonged and verbose presentation, and to explain why some descriptive sections have necessitated the use of comparative portrayals that might, if not forewarned, cause offence to some readers.

The next chapter introduces some of the subjects which make this a distinct and perhaps unusually controversial composition. However, from the way that the media's news reports are, if slowly at present, increasingly displaying evidence of:

- (a) The arguably unstoppable collapse of placidity and contentment around the world;
- (b) The national financial breakdowns which result from borrowing more than can be repaid and afforded;
- (c) The growing climatic instability;
- (d) The dustbowls downstream from where river water is dammed and redirected;
- (e) Expanding terrorism;
- (f) Religious focussing on extreme faiths whilst placid beliefs shrink;
- (g) The blindly unaccepted crisis that the overpopulation/diminishing resources conundrum is giving rise to.

(And the list goes on and on), then judging from the way that all of these issues and many more are typical items in our daily news, it's about time that they are put into their proper perspective. Interpreted, if you like, for what they really are, symptoms of a malaise which could be terminal!

So why haven't we seen this coming crisis before? Two reasons. The first is that such individually distressing matters are becoming almost a daily part of our news and, although any one of them might have caused uproar a few decades ago, they are now just tiresome talking points for a day or two. Second, they are not things which those who have most to lose by exposure would want to make known, are they? Hence it is a norm of safe politics to keep things hidden or discreetly camouflaged where possible. Well, wouldn't you do the same thing?

If that has whet your appetite then, rest assured, there's a lot more in this text that might really give good cause for concern.

Chapter 2

The Urgency and the Current Significance

A rationalised view drawing attention to the urgency and need for action

So why now? Why should any of these subjects warrant a new and radical study at this particular time? Well, in the case of the issues which have a religious content (and that applies to more matters than might be thought at this point), there are two main factors;

(a) There are thought to be certain factions which have only recently managed to acquire access to the source of potentially lethal weapons, whose devotees, it has to be remembered, are quite prepared to forfeit their own lives in order that their impact on less-extreme, civilised society is accomplished with the maximum degree of damage, distress and political repercussions;

(b) It is a long-overdue response to the uprisings and instability that are breaking out, not just in the Middle East and Africa now, but within a new range of different areas around our fatigued planet and;

(c) We are entering an era when the traditional stories we were brought up to believe in without question are becoming increasingly suspect.

Clearly, at one time such tales would have been the only fulfilling or understandable explanations for a multitude of the then-unanswerable questions, but today it's different. In the modern world, scientific, medical, geological, DNA-profiling and similarly expanding disciplines firmly confine increasingly more of those long-standing and traditional religious tales and conjectures into new and completely different contexts. But not a lot of people wish to know that: it's the culture and the comfort of letting sleeping dogs lie. However, in just the same way as Darwin's very unpopular evolution argument, the supporting evidence accumulated and Darwin's case gradually became irrefutable to all but the most obstinate. The case for a serious reappraisal of traditional thinking will eventually prevail; it's just a matter of time against obstinacy.

This is all part of the previously mentioned malady. When a disease of such gravity strikes any society already suffering with self-concealed symptoms of the cancer of overpopulation, where there are more metaphorical mouths to be fed than the resources are able to support, then the resulting, and growing, malignancy can only have terminal results.

So, how does religion come into the formula? Well, imagine yourself as part of an overcrowded, impoverished third-world economy, with no law or social security to protect you and with only your own means to exist on. Place yourself in that situation. Inevitably hungry and probably cold, with a large family to support, and only the spiritual solace of a forlorn and desperately hoped-for comfortable afterlife to look forward to as the only form of hope. Then it is understandable why the embracing church is resorted-to with the strength and trust of resignation. However, inherent with such despair is an obvious vulnerability to exploitation by any ruthless gurus of that faith. It is a case of the needy being open to the "nothing to be lost" culture which facilitates the evils of war and terrorism. Recall, if you will, the much-vaunted "holy war", "ethnic cleansing", "chosen to carry out a Divine Assignment" idioms, and then doesn't it all jigsaw together?

At this point in what might seem to be a challenging manuscript, it is an opportune moment to emphasise that none of us can say with absolute certainty that which other people tell us is true. Whether it is read from any printed script, or whether the teller is on an ornate rostrum, dressed up in jewel-encrusted gown and reading from a leather-bound volume, or if it is just an account from an ordinary guy leaning against a bar, then the information, the instructions or the glorifying rhetoric is only as factual as the speaker or the writer of the account wants it to be, or thinks it to be in the best understanding of the day. But, importantly, as far as historical descriptions are concerned, the fact that an albeit sincere belief or assumption is of simple and unsophisticated origin, and has been recorded without any method of confirmation, surely means that it is no more factual than the tall story that the guy at the bar is trying to spin. In fact, as all this prehistoric narration has been passed on by word-of-mouth for many decades before being written down (writings can be modified too), it really doesn't carry a lot by way of guaranteed authenticity, at least, not to anyone with a sense of reality.

So, if that which has been ordained as a fact is, after reconsideration in the light of impartial, intelligent study, logically concluded to be at least questionable, then is it not a virtuous and morally correct move to acknowledge that a previous 'opinion' was not a fact at all? That restated narratives are utterly fallible. If this is information which has been stated as 'fact' then, surely, it is nothing more than conditioning of a vulnerable mind.

But the object of this section is this: life is a process of learning. Throughout our educations we learn about matters we were either not aware of, or that we might have incorrectly surmised. Of course, there might be some things that we'd been wrongly informed about in all innocence. This happens all the time. It's no disgrace to accept a tale or account as true, especially if it is has been told in sincerity by someone trusted. That, though, is what education is all about: the assimilation of new knowledge and the correction of old where necessary. The only sadness is to witness how many ostensibly intelligent folk simply will not listen to anything other than that which common sense should tell them is, at best, fallible. The enlightened must inevitably be a wiser individual, and this would be especially meaningful if a lifelong conviction has been rationally put into a logical perspective. Enough about mind-changing for now. This will be studied in more depth at a later juncture.

Back to the overpopulation issue. Unbelievably ignored or put to one side by the majority, the gravity of this impending crisis is heightened by the reprehensible fact that it is deliberately being concealed from the populace by those in influential and controlling positions who ought to know better. These people, either for personal or political reasons, avoid the inevitable, profession-prejudicing upset of disclosure by taking the easy way out. They simply keep schtoom and leave the predicament to intensify as it continues along its lethal course. But is it not unsurprising that they choose this alternative? Put yourself in their shoes. Would you relish facing your electorates' reaction when the essentiality of mandatory control of needless reproduction was declared and applied?

Can you imagine the "civil disobedience" and trying to control the virtually inevitable insurrection or even anarchy? Once again, it's a case of the let sleeping dogs lie, (or the 'Cosythink Culture'), but it doesn't mean that the dog isn't becoming more restless with passing time.

This scenario frighteningly alludes to a 'Big Brother' world, but something of that horrifying scale is absolutely unavoidable if – *when* – the mineral, food and water resources run out or cannot meet the sustenance-demands of the population. Now, fault these predictions if you can. If there's even a chance that they're authentic, then we've got some serious problems to sort out. If this book conveys a sense of desperation, now you know why.

Not comfortable reading? Maybe, but that doesn't make it any less plausible or diminish its importance in any way. That is the purpose of this introduction, to prepare the reader for some unadorned and unpleasant facts of life. No less vital, it places some of the pseudo-comforting fantasies that are well past their use-by date into a realistic context. It also lays down the groundwork for highlighting some dilemmas which we seem to be sleepwalking into. It rationalises the background, the development and the basic viability of several concepts that the reader might find and agree would seem to be partly or wholly responsible for the coming crises. It offers conclusions from some inhibition-free thinking (and the validity of such a bombastic and extravagant claim is furnished later). All this and much, much more is in the writing that's ahead, which is presented with the optimistic aim of convincingly suggesting, some ideas which might at least prepare us in some beneficial way. It's not an easy task trying to put all of this highly controversial matter into a reader-friendly composition, whilst presenting some clearly distasteful issues as comprehensively and as unambiguously as possible. It's a huge, uphill quest. This might only be a little drum, but someone's got to bang it as loudly and conspicuously as possible.

Chapter 3

If Demand Exceeds Supply, Reform or Perish

Prospects of world and national overpopulation, and the penalty of ignorance.

It might be sensible to open this contentious survey with the less emotive of the two main concerns to be studied: overpopulation. Surprised or alarmed? Have a look at the numbers. The official, declared estimate of the population in late 2011 is over seven billion – seven thousand millions.

Even more shocking is the declaration by Sir David Attenborough in a recent BBC documentary: "There are three times as many people on this Earth as there were when I started broadcasting sixty years ago." This really puts the crisis into perspective. Three times as numerous, and in just six decades! Think for a moment about those figures. At that rate (which has to be surmised) in just another sixty years less than a normal lifetime, about three times the quantity of our fast-depleting resources will have to be gleaned from somewhere in order to feed, house and sustain the world's population. Consider, also, the current level of adequacy, with vast masses near starvation!

'From somewhere?' What sort of fantasy is that? 'Somewhere' simply doesn't exist. We might complain about austerity measures and difficult belt-tightening with real-term incomes decreasing against family expenditure, but in the UK we've got it easy! If the news and documentary broadcasts are to be believed, then there are more and more areas around the world where land can no longer bear cereals, where rivers and still-reachable aquifers are drying up , and we are having to go to increasingly rigorous and costly lengths just in order to reach oil that isn't politically exploitable. Not only that, but these figures and dark depictions don't take into account the extent of our existing environmental and ecological deterioration. There are problems which will soon be making themselves manifest as a direct result of

(a) The growing pollution-sourced environmental desecration with

(b) The impact of the relentlessly destabilising and progressively more damaging weather;

(c) The direct and indirect effects of the recently discovered ozone layer's frailty and breakdown.

(d) The rising level of the sea as glaciers and ice-caps unstoppably melt into the oceans;

(e) The unfreezing permafrost's virtually uncontrollable release of methane gas, which accelerates global warming.

The vicious circle continues, as more repercussions come to light.

As we proceed through the second decade of the new century, there is steadily more evidence of potentially cataclysmic financial collapses around the world. This is downplayed by the government, but several nations are already pleading poverty and begging for help. Such collapses usually emanate from either a ruthless protectorate's greed or, more often, the short-sighted governmental exploit of appealing to their electorate by sweetening the nation's finances with un-meetable loans. It's not only the governments of poorer countries which go to such term-length exploits. So, why do the elected representatives of more and more economies allow their systems to get into such a state? At the risk of stating the obvious, in any democracy the government secures favourable election results by either materially providing its electorate with an enhanced level of security, lifestyle and comfort, so there is nothing to be gained by voting for the opposition party; or, if times should be a little more difficult, then promises (not always honoured, of course) have to be relied upon. The opposition party does not have to provide the above comforts, just to publicise how the governing side is financing them and to try and convince the electorate that borrowing under them will be lower and conditions will improve. That's how democracy works: by persuading the voters with inducements and promises.

The loans that normally have to be borrowed in order to achieve these enticements usually have to be honoured by the new, voted-in party. In other words, the victorious party has to honour election pledges without making obvious shortages and this is usually achieved by borrowing. It's like a game, almost, so is it really surprising that we're in financial shtook? Logically it's only a matter of time before, one after the other, the world's economies run dry. As we can see, the rot has already set in as the string of acclaim-seeking governments with their exchequers casually taking for granted that massive credits can be borrowed from a bottomless pot, have discovered that loans have to be repaid! No longer can extravagant advances be blindly called on to cover mounting expenses. The global dilemma means that it's pay-back time. If there's no surplus, capital or other resources to honour the debt then, as Greece, Ireland, Spain, Portugal etc. have so humiliatingly discovered, out comes the begging-bowl. The UK was only recently in danger of taking that route, and it's not much better now.

However, although it appears that it needed the example of others' degradation before our unaffordable spending was reined-in as well as possible without revolution, there are still many who prefer to turn a blind eye to the harsh alternative. This particular imprudence presents an important analogy that will, it is hoped, be seen to apply to the basic message of this writing. But I digress.

Back to the ongoing train of dilemmas which keep appearing. Is it not obvious that, as things stand, the deteriorating compound global situation can only continue to slide down the slippery slope towards subsistence-deficiency and consequent social breakdown? The consequences of that don't bear thinking about! But they will.

How dismaying it is to see how many of us just don't seem to care about the impending disaster? It's almost as if we are intent on denying that there *is* a problem. We cannot carry on feeding and providing more and more with less and less. Is it a vacuous hope that it will all, somehow, just resolve itself? Perhaps some sort of divine power will magically appear to 'make things alright again'? Any bells ringing?

In our self-satisfied, comfortably complacent western world it is all too easy to pooh-pooh austere reports about the growing overpopulations, shortages and predicaments in less-affluent areas with scornful dismissals: "Oh, that's all in the distant future and 'they' will have it all sorted-out before long" or the often-heard but irresponsible "It's 'their' problem, not ours". Perhaps we reject any concern with a sanctimonious "It's not for us to tell 'them' to limit the size of 'their' families!" These dismissive brush-offs sound familiar, perhaps. Also, there is another often-heard comment with a more insightful sentiment, which provides a clear warning about the complexity and sheer gravity of this coming Armageddon. It makes the quite valid point that in those places without any social welfare, having a large family is not only virtually unavoidable, but it is also the best guarantee that parents are able to procure for their own support in their declining and probably dependent years. This clearly balances ethics against the instinct for self-preservation, which is a major stumbling-block when the possibility of compulsory restrictions (such as in China) are considered, particularly if a country's economy cannot afford to take on the support of their senior citizens, surfacing in ever increasing rates, and it will take several generations before it stabilises numerically.

That's a global, long-term, pessimistic outlook, though. The national circumstances in the near future have to be put into perspective first, particularly those that are quite possible to revise and will then be self-sustaining. The pivotal hurdle to be overcome is our personal, and collective, recognition that there is a problem. The temptation, probably natural, is to sidestep the issue with a dismissive "why should *we* concern ourselves about something that isn't really affecting us at the moment? We've got all that we need. Our children are well-fed, educated and safe and, even if they *should* have trouble finding employment and earning a living when they grow up, then our Social Security system will ensure that they are able to live comfortable lives and raise families of their own". If that isn't a mindless self-perpetuating recipe for social disintegration, then what is? At the risk of accusations of being a prophet of doom, how can more and more *possibly* exist on less and less?

Just recall how many times sentiments similar to these have been expressed to you. Have you not readily agreed with them? They appear in a very different light if one makes the effort to think about them logically, when they are put into perspective against the growing-population/diminishing-resources statistics? Doesn't such rationalisation reveal that such opinions are, in fact, short-sighted and lacking in analysis? With all the evidence in the media, we cannot be other than aware about the growing disparity as world population rises and energy/agricultural/financial/fresh water reserves drain away; also, how aggressively unsettled our planet is becoming. It doesn't require a great deal of intellectual competence to see and anticipate the ultimate conclusion. It's our failure to *recognise* what's ahead of us that is the hurdle.

Rubbing it in, perhaps, but needs must; is it not fundamentally disturbing to conclude that nobody wants to concede? But what do people do? Ignore it? Pretend it's not there or that it will sort itself out? How mature is that? In short, the above responses and opinions are symptomatic of an unthinking mindset: of those who either prefer not to accept facing something in life which might be disagreeable by dissociating themselves from it (we're probably all able to recall one or two such people), or of those who are simply incapable of working out the basic plus-and-minuses of non-sustainability, however obvious it all might be!

The second group we can only feel sorry for, but with the first it's another matter.

Surely, if the facts are laid out and are easily provable, and if these proven facts confirm that there's a disaster ahead unless we do something about it, then is it not a case of virtual suicide, or of being instrumental in hazarding the lives of our offspring, if we ignore it? Putting it another way, those of us who are able to work out the consequences of an impasse surely must carry some degree of culpability if they *consciously* do nothing to make their concerns known? It is this self-suppression that has to be recognised before anything can be done to tackle the problem itself. Doesn't that sound like good sense? After all, it's our future and that of coming generations which is under threat. Nothing could possibly be more important than that! Think about it please.

Harsh words, maybe, but the utter gravity of the situation justifies them so that the next move can be sought.

Now the decisiveness of this issue has been successfully illustrated, some of the more intimate details can be elaborated on . Before that, however, there is a grave issue which has to be confronted: a matter with acute arithmetical connotations. This is the conundrum of more and longer-living elders needing the support and benefits that are paid for by fewer taxable workers and the diminishing trade in national exports. In other words, even if the birth rate can successfully be brought under control, then in just twenty years or so, the majority of the populace will be approaching or have reached their retirement and pension/benefit-maintained age. They will expect to live longer, they might well have their offspring living at home and as such will only partially covered by benefits. This growing financial liability will have to be carried by a proportionately-shrinking (thanks to technology) number of taxpayers. It might be an obvious question, but with more people becoming 'benefit-reliant' by the day and the less-work-to-be-done/fewer taxpayers quandary providing less funds with which the national economy can or is able to provide for the longer-living and numerically-snowballing pensioners, then from where is all this expenditure going to come?

Obvious circumstances, simple question, unarguable mathematics, enormous enigma. Yet another impasse, maybe, but nothing like as terminal as that of the population/resources deadlock.

So how can we afford or even *dare* to ignore the prodigious magnitude of this overpopulation predicament for any longer? , Or the way that some of us are continuing to blindly snub or disregard the horrible inevitability of the catastrophic disaster that is on its way? The evidence is there to be seen. So is evidence of the corruption that is becoming normal among not only the top echelons, but also the staff of newspapers, the police, television companies, councils, political parties, hospitals, banks and financial institutions, even care homes. I could go on, but doesn't it all reflect the festering insecurity of our world? If you think about it, it all originates back to more people than the economy can accommodate. Like it or not, that is what many regard as the big unmentionable: overpopulation.

The evidence is there to be seen. Now it's time to think outside the box.

Chapter 4

How and Why Certain Statistics are Manipulated

Unemployment figures: reasons for their misrepresentation and how it's done

Still think that there's really nothing much for us to worry about? Try looking at the situation from a different viewpoint. Here in the U.K., the government utilises its declared unemployment figures. Although wavering about a bit might not be particularly alarming now in early 2014, this regular monthly publication of these specific figures and the direction of their drift is the gauge by which the public assesses or evaluates our *status quo*. In other words, just how comfortable we are as an economic entity. When we are told that unemployment figures are climbing people start to get restless, worrying about their own job-security. The unemployed, in turn, worry how much more out-of-reach any hope of employment is becoming. Put another way, it's an important indicative warning to the public about more-people-than-work, and has an obvious connection to the symptom which the politicians are trying to avoid at all costs: overpopulation. Nobody wants to think about overpopulation. Politicians, using their common sense, with their own careers and self-interest at heart, avoid using the word at all costs. They keep overpopulation out of the picture by manipulating unemployment figures to appear as low as possible, as will be shown.

Governments don't like confrontation. They like to say what their electorate wants to hear. With elections and personal incomes in mind, they do their very best to pander to the national complacency factor. One of the principal ways they do this is to discreetly adjust unemployment figures. As these have quite significant reassurance value, it might be sensible to conduct a close study of the credibility and validity of these statistics. Statistics, don't forget, that are both compiled and presented to us by the offices which are most impacted by the public's reaction to them. There are several methods by which figure 'refinements' are brought about, so let's examine them in turn.

First, unemployment figures. As a basic principle, these should be the calculated difference between the number of people who are physically free and available for taxable employment nationally, and the number of those who are actually in work. A somewhat simplified way of illustrating this is to consider if the national economics equate so that the number of the available workforce is greater than those who are "gainfully employed", then this difference constitutes the monthly-declared Unemployment Figure. In effect, those who are employed have to support those who are not.

If this Unemployment Figure (or the disparity) is fairly small, then this difference can normally be accommodated quite comfortably. But in a situation where unemployment statistics are considerable, the cost of financing the demand for support measures can become significant. As a direct consequence of untenable disparity between figures, budget adjustments and spending cuts would have to be initiated – not an electorate-friendly measure. Alternately, national resources would have to be sought, or more monetary loans acquired, made available and tapped-into in order to cover this disbursement.

This might appear simplistic, but there are sound reasons for making it so: first, the impact this monthly depiction has on the man in the street is often only of secondary interest, but the subconscious influence upon the public is more important. Rather than just a number, unemployment figures affect the underlying national stability factor: how securely we stand as a member of the compound world society. The evidence is there. When unemployment rises, so does social disruption. So is it not common sense for the office presenting the figures to the public to discreetly massage them to be as reassuring as possible? How they do that will be shown. The second reason is the increasing workforce numbers, through population increase, immigration, and decreasing need for labour due to steadily advancing technology, computer-use and efficiency, the diminishing revenue from the leisure industry as funds tighten, and so on. All told, it is inevitable that the number available for employment increases with time, and no matter what measures are taken to conceal them for as long as possible, it is an unavoidable reality that increasing unemployment is an uncontainable certainty of modern life, an arithmetical product from the above ingredients. Can it be more clearly illustrated than that?

A direct consequence of the above is the equally inescapable issue about the population/work availability impasse that, sooner or later, will place our economy in a wretched and unsustainable economical overload: outgoing costs of essential imports, fuel and energy, benefit payments and loan-sourced repayments inevitably spiralling. These will no longer be able to be matched by national revenues and reserves, which could result in even more borrowing, the last straw which will finally break the camel's back! Inescapable yes, but is it insuperable? Probably not now. But soon?

All this could mean that we can look forward to living in a society where the few of us who are fortunate enough to be employed will, as a mathematical certainty, have to be taxed progressively more exorbitantly in order that the unemployed can be funded. The latter, disillusioned souls living on meagre, minimum handouts and existing with little or no dignity or self-esteem, who'll have nothing materially to lose whatever they do, who will be the enigma of this equation. Their unwarranted predicament and associated state of mind is the grave psychological outcome which grows more distressing with time. All very disturbing, but it is the untenability of the coming crisis which needs to be emphatically placed in its proper and unvarnished perspective. That done, it must be broadcast so that it is recognised for what it is, before anyone will break their own complacent comfort bubble, bite the bullet and do something about it.

Again looking at this horrible scenario from a political viewpoint, it is natural that official unemployment statistics are taken as the widely-accepted thermometer by which the nation's welfare and confidence in the soundness of the elected government's policies is judged. It is quite evident, then, why certain ministry departments might be tempted to covertly manipulate the monthly unemployment figures so they appear to be as low, and hence as reassuring, as possible. That's their job, and with the nation's placidity (as well as their own careers, often) at stake, it is quite understandable why they might avoid disclosing any non-essential ugly truths which could cause dissent? After all, no political party wins popularity and votes with bad news of an approaching crisis.

But this is where the matter of declared and actual employment statistics comes in. The impression of those figures is significantly and favourably enhanced if school-leavers are enticed or expected to spend several years of their normal working life at university, and not on the unemployment register. In order to qualify for admission, however, suitably high examination results have to be achieved to sort the wheat from the chaff, so that only candidates with the academic capacity and genuine ambition to justify the not-insignificant expense further education demands, are selected and accepted.

To this observer, however, it appears that virtually every school leaver manages to achieve at least a pass, if not the all-singing all-dancing honours grades which nowadays seem to be the norm. Do any students fail these exams? Having been educated in an age when reaching an academic standard high enough to be acceptable for university consideration was no mean achievement, I might be forgiven for making an observation about this modern inconsistency.

School leaving examinations are basically nothing more than academic tests by which the better students are segregated from the others. One might even venture to submit that it's a principle whereby all students who take this written test obtain a certificated personal degree or gauge of their intellectual capacity, which is then compared against those of other students and the arithmetical comparisons would positively divulge their relative astuteness.

I should clarify that I am not rebuking students; far from it. It is the cruelly exploitative and morally-contentious social principle itself and the shameful covering-up manoeuvres that the students are merely taking advantage of! Students leave school with just two options: to seek employment somewhere, probably joining a long queue of all the hopefuls in very adverse, overcrowded conditions, usually unsuccessfully, which results in the notorious dole queue and the unemployment register; or to seek higher education at a university with all the prestige that goes with it. The second option might only defer the day that they have to join the queue at the job centre, but the queue will be even longer and the queuers even more disillusioned.

But this second option holds an obvious appeal for the school-leaver. How much more consoling for the egos it is to be 'studying for a degree at university' than 'looking for a position with the right requirements' or 'there just don't seem to be the vacancies that would be suitably fulfilling' or other unconvincing disclaimers. Additionally, there's the appeal of the student club culture that's synonymous with groups of perfectly normal, like-minded, high-spirited, pleasure-seeking and somewhat incautious life discoverers respond to the need to prove themselves to the world and their mates. How much more appealing this is as opposed to the drudgery of seeking employment!

In any case, from the point of view of the school-leaver, there is virtually nothing to be lost by choosing this second option. Reducing it all to basic realism the university regime is an effortless and inviting route to follow. From the political point of view, it's a case of one more student into the flourishing further education system, one less unit on the unemployment statistics for a few years, whilst parents and student enjoy a degree of self-respect. This provides reassurance to all those who have been manipulated, whilst the Employment Office defers the one new registration unit probably many thousands of times over, and likely leaves for the next government to sort out.

As mentioned earlier, it doesn't take a lot of in-depth analysis to decipher the purpose of the government's strategy, both from a psychological and an economical point of view. It is nothing less than a case of political exploitation of personal and family image., It is a deferral of the inevitable and reflective employment difficulties that are incumbent with newly-subsidising and managing a not-insignificant section of the electorate. This system of subtle financial doctoring delegates school-leavers away from benefits and on to repayable loans and/or the support of the students' families. It is a way of absorbing the many, many thousands of otherwise-unemployed people who provide, not only education, but all the supporting maintenance, office, catering and other ancillary roles, not to mention the businesses that depend on the property's and the students' outgoings and spending.

Bearing in mind the extent of the collateral spin-off and its inherent impact on expenditure, political image and the resulting overpopulation, it is easy to see why the government might be sorely tempted to conceal it all in just the same way? Whilst in speculative mode: if you happened to be a school-leaver, wouldn't you be thankful that you could make use of such an obviously ludicrous, governmentally face-saving farce?

Chapter 5

Collateral Costs and Potential Prudence

Our university system, the covert economical and psychological manoeuvres

The contention in the previous chapter might require a little further explanation as it is quite accusative and might not be easily acknowledged without some measure of further scrutiny. However, there is no room for any ambiguities with an issue of this magnitude and possibly, as such, it demands some frank and business-like analysis. It calls into question the continuation of the university structure, a hugely expensive compound administration in its current form.

First, let's look at its productive value i.e. the quantity and quality of the system's productive output balanced against the amalgamated time, effort and expense to achieve this outcome. Without access to various University statistics, and wishing to present the relevant facts so they can be given credence to without reference to unconfirmed statistics, one has only to utilise the evidence that can be seen all around us. It doesn't take a penetrating degree of observation to be very aware of the abundance of youngsters who proudly proclaim that they are "At uni., studying for a degree in [something or other]" or a similarly-impressive declaration. Neither can it pass unheeded just how many graduates with stunning academic qualifications proceed directly from university to the local job centre! Nor can it pass unmentioned that some of the disciplines that have been studied for years are of dubious or absolutely no relevance or real value in today's world!

This portrayal doesn't apply to all. Unfortunately, it does apply to the majority. It is only a minority, however the crème de la crème of students from here and around the world, who are fortunate enough to get themselves into one of the consummate houses of education, where they study, graduate and are quickly scooped-up by industry or other institutions as recognition and a consequence of their advanced education. That's how it should be, but not how it is, where use of the university epithet is exploited in order to conceal for a few years, a virtually countless multitude of partly-deceived, partly-exploiting young people who would probably otherwise be on the unemployment register. This is a flagrant, almost criminal abuse of our much-vaunted university institution that calls out to be examined. The idiosyncrasy we have to censure amounts to an underhand and covert political exploitation of that which is, and must remain as, our globally-acclaimed further education structure. It must not be polluted and made an object of ridicule for political purposes. Reflect on our history of education and the situation now.

Only a decade or two ago, British academic qualifications were testimony of an intellectual integrity to match all. Now it appears that, to put it bluntly, our university entry-standards have been lowered so radically that anyone who can hold a pencil and put a tick in a box achieves the much-televised, shock-faced "I've PASSED!" and joins the others at "uni". This might be a little colourful, but it does serve to graphically illustrate how our system has been trashed, by gradually allowing more and more school-leavers through our universities to keep them off the unemployment register. Whilst in full knowledge of the burden that it merely postpones, our successive politicians have actively debased our university system. But it hasn't been easy for them! They've had to dream up utterly trivial courses to accommodate the possibly academically-challenged, and to organise low-cost loans to make things easier. This is another example of the 'deferment' ploy, this time with the loan-repayments. So we can see how valuable the strategy to keep school-leavers out of the job centre is. But the politicians are happy that they've artificially kept the unemployment figures down, the students are happy that they've got themselves a prestigious position for a while, the parents are happy that their kids are not on the dole, and inescapable matters that will ultimately have to be confronted are postponed. So, like a disease without treatment, it's left to become increasingly septic. This pantomime will continue for as long as the public wants to be deceived. Is the discomfort of facing the facts really that intolerable? And what about morals?

Saying that the public *wants* to be deceived might need to be validated. Have you ever had reason to research, or even to casually question he employment statistics' public perception in this light? Or how and why the figures are manipulated to maintain the public's secure image, or how the far-reaching university con psychologically exploits the majority of those caught up in it, and all the other issues that have been raised in the preceding chapters? Then if the answer is the expected one, would you ask yourself why you've never questioned it. Could it not be a direct result of the phoney comfort these tactics create? If there's no obvious reason to look outside the comfort box, then he who is cosy makes sure that he stays inside it!

Back to the matter of productive value. At the risk of stating the obvious, if the universities' intake numbers were slashed by simply reverting entry-grades to higher academic standards, then applicants would be identified with a higher level of intellectual ability and a genuine ambition and initiative to productively utilise the universities' expensive tutorials and administrations. In that way, the dead wood would be eliminated, allowing a more intense focus on the higher-calibre students who deserve it, thus raising the success rate. The pedigree of subsequent graduates would be reflected in their qualifications' value to any potential employers.

But productive value does not only utilise the quality and quantity of a system's output; it also reflects the input. This is a balance that depends fundamentally on disbursement expenses. The amount of effort expended in attaining entry would of course influence the system's working efficiency. This is where the elimination of all the dead wood comes in. Observing the present system as an outsider, I would hypothesise that the non-productive, benefit-bound portion of the University student quota accounts for about 80% of those who currently enter our universities. On a simple numerical basis, is it not perfectly feasible, then that between half and three-quarters of the institutions for higher education could be dispensed with? This includes not only the multitude of lecturers and teaching staff, but also a large contingent of campus maintenance staff, administration, accounting and office personnel, and the often huge and extensive buildings themselves. With a little modification, think of the much-needed domestic potential that could be gained. On a national scale, the savings and the social benefits that could be achieved by cutting-out the superfluous university dead wood, although they would be enormous, might very well be negated by the support liabilities of those on benefit as a result of these measures and enforcements. But the bulk of the new cost to the economy would be support for those who would have to be provided for in a few years' time anyway!

So, let's think about it all from the moral aspect. Take this analogy: woodland floors are brown, dead and virtually lifeless (except in spring, when the leafless canopy allows the light in for a few, precious weeks and the bluebells can flourish). Whenever the superfluous trees are cut back or removed the light-starved topsoil virtually explodes into all sorts of life which benefits and flourishes as a result. It's the same with our education system. If the superfluous, wasteful elements are re-sited where they ought to be, then the suppressed elements can benefit and thrive in the consequently focussed attention. This presents a dramatic picture of a measure which would result in unwelcome effects and painful remedies. But life-saving surgery usually does.

This is the onerous and complex problem which needs so desperately to be faced. It calls for measures which nobody wants to put their signature to! Not only would all the unproductively-accommodated students be unloaded onto the dole queue, but so would all the now-redundant staff-members from the newly-empty and surplus universities that would, as a result, be redundant and abandoned. As might some of the residents in the area: shop owners and suppliers who do so well from the students' and staff's custom. Such collateral damage is, I am sure, part of the reason for the cover-up.

In summary of an unpleasant chapter: if the artificially-inflated university culture were to be rationalised down to regain its healthy, efficient and educationally-meaningful standard, with all the otherwise-unemployed students no longer able to enjoy their counterfeit break from reality and the now-surplus staff and knock-on supporting personnel being relegated with the students on to the unemployment register, then just imagine the extent and the size of the cost-penalty and the burden that the nation's Benefit budget would suddenly have to carry. Not only that, but we're already lumbered with a trillion-pound deficit. In the light of all this gloom, is it really surprising that the university system is being exploited in this way? More to the point, that this ostensible duplicity is being concealed from the public for as long as the politicians think that they can get away with it? So, once again, and bearing in mind the election-popularity factor, if you were wearing a politician's hat, wouldn't you be very tempted to take precisely the same course?

Chapter 6

More "Sleight of Hand" Intrigues

How part-time employees and pointless "Quangos" are used to mislead us

Part-time employees. Whatever might be thought about the principle of sharing work and income, the bare facts of the part-timer situation are that one full-time employee will, as far as productivity is concerned, be about as work-efficient as approximately two or three part-time employees paid to do the same job. There are, of course, factors other than pay which make a full-time employee more advantageous to a company: issues like there being two or three times the likelihood of sick leave or other cause of absence from work. But if an employer can be persuaded to trade off one of his full-time employees and take on two or three part-timers to do comparable work, then the number of people on the register claiming unemployment benefit is reduced by up to as many as three in each case. That might not sound like a lot, but hasn't it become conspicuous how the number of part-timers in supermarkets and shops have multiplied? If you multiply that number by the number of such visible instances, it must run into hundreds of thousands, which doesn't take into account the number of part-timers who have out-of-sight positions.

Now, this writing is not in any way demeaning to those who have part-time jobs. On the contrary, like the students in the previous chapter, it is the deplorable political exploitation of the system that is being criticised. Students and part-timers are merely taking advantage of the only real option open to them. As said, this is more evidence of the way that the facts of our crumbling situation are being concealed.

How about all those "quangos" then? That rash of absolutely unnecessary jobs, each one devised just "...to conceal the failure of another"? This and the following quotations provide revelations about some really frightening statistics concerning apparently misleading measures, were recently divulged in a terrifying programme entitled "Britain's Trillion-Pound Horror Story". This 90-minute eye-opener is both utterly shocking and comprehensively revealing, and has to be seen more than once before the extent of the covert and underhand duplicity that it so bravely reveals can be acknowledged and believed. Of course, there's no way that all the facts that this programme lays bare can be relayed in this book. The focal section of the programme was to invincibly describe how many pseudo jobs are fabricated to support other inefficient and effectively unsustainable fields of work, most of which are themselves concocted to buoy up other nonsensical missions. It brought into frightening focus the governmental conspiracy and the absolute maelstrom of useless, bureaucratically-devised and integrated positions, each reliant upon one or more of the others for its basic significance. Singly or accumulatively, these organisations create no practical or material product whatsoever!

These quangos could be eliminated with little, if any, loss, other than a substantial increase in the unemployment numbers, of course.

"Britain's Trillion Pound Horror Story" went on to name very specifically some examples of fallacious occupations, including some in the police and nursing sectors. However, it was ostensibly education-orientated organisations, carrying job-titles such as "Early Years Inclusion Facilitation", "Training to Gain", "Early Learning Partnerships", "Learning Outside the Classroom", "The Children's Plan", "National Skills Academy" plus "The Framework for Personal Learning and Thinking Skills" which were found to be particularly jaundiced.

It doesn't take a great deal of perception to work out the purpose and the politics of this shady charade, or to visualise how many of these positions of employment could be concocted in this illusionary way in order to furtively provide impressive-sounding openings that occupy people who would otherwise be enlarging the unemployment statistics. Clearly, jobs with no productive purpose and innumerable members of staff being employed to achieve this imaginary outcome, it's not difficult to realise the political reasons for these pointless positions' being fabricated. Neither is it difficult to see how masquerades such as these demonstrate how politics can be manipulated to provide false figures and images. Such positions of employment are an obvious benefit from the political point of view, and we certainly cannot blame the individuals who are employed in these fallacious posts. They're just taking advantage of a job which has been offered to them.

Back to those unemployment figures and their surreptitious falsifying, engineering and concealment. The next scam which needs to be highlighted is that of the (inevitably popular with the public) ongoing prolongation of "maternity leave" concessions.

Now, putting ethics aside for a moment, whatever one might think about the basic morality of someone taking on a "permanent" position of employment whilst actively planning to start a family, it is smaller employers who invariably suffer when their staff continuity is upset. When an essential member of staff places an employer in a position of having to find and train a part-time worker to the same level of competence. This is often a gamble for there is often a lot to be forfeited, (a) on the substitute part-time employee having the capability to smoothly take over the responsibility without disrupting the company's flow, and (b) remain reliably in this placement for the duration of the "permanent" employee's absence. Often, this will occur for increasingly more months almost at the absentee's own discretion! So, already subjected to being probably overstretched by the legal obligation to "Keep the position open to be returned to" for mothers (whatever the cost and impracticality that might be involved with having to take-on a temporary stand-in), the disrupted small company now has to accommodate a similar burden with the new "Paternity Leave" liability. One might protest in favour of human rights, but doesn't the wage-paying employer have any rights? For example, reliable returns and attendance in return for his reliably-furnished salary, or the right not to have to take on unknown and possibly unreliable temporary workers when he could, with far less production-disruption, simply replace a disappearing employee. Perhaps the right to negotiate with female and/or male birth-influenced staff about whether any flexi-time compromises could be arranged to accommodate disturbances and adjustments, particularly so as the full-time employee who is concerned might not be suffering from any work-restrictive malady.

No doubt there are other less obvious, 'concessions' being utilised to conceal the effective-vs-virtual unemployment figures from the public each month: the university canopy, the part-timers manipulations, that subversive 'quango' ruse, leave-concession disruptions and so on. Each of these tactics can so easily be confirmed as cover. They are conceived and implemented specifically so that the real unemployment situation and its true figures are hidden from the public. Shades of concealing the 'Big O' (overpopulation)?

So the next question is what would be the true unemployment figure without these political adjustments? We can only hazard a guess. I wouldn't mind betting that in real terms, i.e. with the university non-starters in their most prudent social position, no permanent/part-timers smokescreens, no exorbitant and uncalled-for leave, no useless quangos and so on, the true unemployment figure would be at least double that which is declared each month. If that statistic didn't spark off a huge overpopulation controversy when announced, what else could any government do to avoid facing this unanswerable conundrum? Nothing. That is why duping the public will continue for as long as they can possibly get away with it.

Bearing in mind how demanding it is for the unemployed (at least, the conscientious unemployed) to find secure work placements in the current economy, with shops and factories closing down by the day, employers having to reduce their headcounts to stay viable, building and estate-markets on go-slow, fewer holidays being taken, holiday company problems and so on, it doesn't require a fortune-teller to predict that however the figures might be massaged ("lies, damn lies, and statistics"), the future for workers doesn't look good.

To close the "concealed unemployment" allegation, I must ask, "what is it they can see that we can't?". Virtually every party political broadcast presents one of our MPs assuring us that their party is absolutely determined to bring down unemployment! or "we are determined to get all those who are able to work back to work" and other uplifting claims.

Perhaps they have a grasp of mathematics that the older generation weren't taught at school, but something doesn't quite add up. Surely, if the total number of jobs available (which, reflected in the course of decreasing industry/workforce needs, must be decreasing) is less than the total number of people seeking them (which, by force of circumstance, is inexorably increasing), anyone who can count must be able to see that any promise based on such a calculation is fantasy: unrealistic, illogical and even dishonest.

But just how devious is all that sleight-of-hand? Some of it is so indirect that it avoids recognition, like extended maternity and paternity leave. It might not at first appear to be anything to do with the overpopulation concealment, but every man-hour lost by leave removes at least one person from the unemployment register. If you multiply that by the number of cases, add a percentage to cover the number of expecting mothers- who, if it were not for this 'leave', simply wouldn't find the employment worthwhile then, in conjunction with all the other stealthy concealments, it all adds up. The unemployment figures are artificially kept lower and the unquestioning public is deceived into thinking there is nothing to be concerned about. As a result of all this fiddling of numbers, the biggest problem of all, the overpopulation factor, doesn't even have to be brought into the picture. As for attending to it as anyone with integrity would, I rest my case.

Chapter 7

The Object of these Manoeuvres

The applied-psychology behind the how and why of misrepresentation

This is a lengthy analysis, but there's more to come, and it doesn't get any easier to digest. But this book is about some very serious issues, and in order that its arguments are plausible and sound, it is absolutely essential that the accuracy of various assertions is questioned and put into a realistic perspective. It is also important that the reasons and motives behind the alleged disparities are seen and accounted for from the viewpoint of those who present these inexactitudes.

I will take the opportunity to summarise some of the contentions which have been made, and make a few points for consideration. We had a brief look at the theory that beliefs based on superseded and factually unreliable stories need to be sensibly reassessed to qualify as impartial opinions, particularly with the wealth of new discoveries and information available.

We have also looked into the disconcerting matter of the local and worldwide overpopulation problem and its virtually inevitable escalation. So far we've taken a glance at the global reasons for the essential (but practically non-existent) concern and the disturbing fact that nobody seems to care about this coming crisis. I aim to bring into focus not only the degree of this heedlessness, but how our successive governments actually exploit this blindness by distorting and manipulating figures and circumstances in order to disguise what they don't relish revealing to the populace. This contention was contextualised in relation to the obviously mounting social and financial insecurity factor, as was the manifest waste of much-needed money to finance these deceptions. So far, so good, but if the plausibility of the opening contentions can be accepted as being at least worth further thought, then I might have partially answered the "how" question. Now, what about "why"? What could be the underlying purpose of these complex manoeuvres and the reason for their cover-up?

Think about it. Think about how you would relish being in a position where you knew about a possible holocaust but, with no conceivable way out of the catastrophe, would you come clean about it? Would you relish the prospect of facing the inevitable public alarm if the cause of our financial weakness and collapsing social security was finally admitted? And make the even more inflammatory admission that there's no feasible answer to it? That this country, just like all the rest of the Earth's collective communities, is reaching the point where it carries more people than it has the means to employ, support and accommodate? Or to have to admit that the population statistics are relentlessly growing without there being any investigation (let alone employment) of a means of sustainable constraint, or a practical method of restraining the birth rate. We are on a no less than suicidal course because of this.

It's simple, logical and natural prudence from a political point of view. Would any political party want to make such a terrible declaration to the electorate? Such news could cause a revolution. Even if it were watered down a little to be fed in small doses, would any vote-conscious faction even consider presenting such bad news to an electorate on whose affinity and vote their position and future might depend? Especially so if it can be hushed up for just a little longer, so that another party might well inherit the potential time bomb after an election. Politicians are human, after all, and if an unsolvable conundrum and the inevitable damaging disruption can be avoided by pretending that the warning signs haven't been seen then that's what they do

But doesn't such a duplicitous situation make it even more understandable that it's being kept out of public sight, and why it will be for as long as the electorate unthinkingly swallows comfort pills; like the unemployment pseudo-statistics, and the pseudo-wealth based on finances no more substantial than recallable loans?

That is another answer to the question "why?" whilst our "trillion-pound horror story" disclosures put our alleged 'wealth' into perspective, and whilst we were proudly able to proclaim a triple-A credit rating. Now, (in early 2014,) this 'advantage' has been withdrawn, meaning that we cannot borrow as much! Now, isn't that a relief?

Just allow yourself a few moments to look around, not so much at the figures that are fed to the gullible public , but at the underlying facts and trends and the sheer inevitability of the increasing demand/resource imbalance. Even before this worldwide inadequacy becomes too manifest to deny, the growing degree of social unrest almost everywhere reflects an underlying awareness (however subliminal) of the situation's imminence! With evidence such as the costs of living, bank and pensions-failures, growth of national debts, the cancerous outbreak of corruption within trusted institutions, the unemployed and benefit-supported and climate change, it's easy to answer "why" the cover up. Many still deny global warming, even as they read about floods, droughts, disappearing glaciers and icecaps and flora and fauna becoming extinct. Why? Because it's too big to handle. Am I a panic-merchant, or just an anxious whistleblower? If you're still not sure, then read on. If there should still be any doubt in the reader's mind about the intensity of the austerity facing us, let's return to the conundrum about overpopulation, and, more to the uncomfortable point, its solution. First, the conflict between natural proliferation and the common sense resolution to control birth rate simply has to be made public. However, this is inconsistent with traditional instincts and, as a result, very easily evaded. Rather, it must be re-emphasised at every opportunity to prevent its being disregarded with time. It will be a long time before it's accepted, however, even if all the alternatives are made clear, even as the situation deteriorates.

The big problem, though, is the immense artificial barrier that has to be overcome before a family limiting its offspring will even be considered.

It is a perfectly natural instinct for a couple to start a family. But why is this? Why should it be "natural", and why should we feel unfulfilled if we don't have children?

It doesn't take a lot of insight to answer those questions, but in the interest of clarity and logical deduction, I will examine them.

Right from the start of our 'thinking' ability, as opposed to when we responded to more primitive instincts like all the other animals, mankind gradually became aware that by having children and those children having children the species would gain strength in numbers and there'd be someone to care for the elders when age restricted their self-support. In any case, proliferation of the species or not, sex was not so much, let's say, "nice" in those times, but an instinct which became conditioned in with evolution and needed to be responded to, (as is alluded-to later). So, over the innumerable generations, as the self-interest, the numerical and social advantages and the monogamous loving developed, alongside our thinking ability, motivation for sexual activity changed.

From the original primitive and spontaneous level of mating (as opposed to "intercourse" – an important difference) in response to different stimuli, as still applies to other life-forms, the human race's developing intellect introduced a new feature into the matter of sex, that of objective and purpose (which, if you think about it, is the pivotal point where we evolved away from the rest of the animal kingdom). That might also be about the time when we discovered the difference between "sex" and "making love", but in the interest of keeping to the point of the notion, we'll leave that evocative conjecture alone for now.

The purpose of this line of reasoning is to address the way in which the human race developed from subliminal species-reliant patterning to achieve our unique capacity to choose the time and/or the purpose for having sex. In other words, how mankind evolved above the "responsive, programmed-in sex for the <u>unwitting</u> species-survival instinct", to having the choice and the ability to enjoy sex just for pleasure's sake. Nevertheless that doesn't mean that all vestiges of the primitive urges just disappeared overnight. After all, the strength and compulsion of this urge perpetuated us and every other species!

Next, there is the question of why we should feel unfulfilled in any way if we don't have children. If you have read the above and can accept that in that past the human race depended 100% upon instinctive urges and impulses, and if you can also appreciate the almost unimaginable power that would have been essential for those subliminally conditioned (and, remember, "purposeless") instincts to have overcome all the natural ecological hazards of that time to result in our species' survival, then it must be quite understandable why some vestiges of these instincts still remain in our psyche. It is the logically nonsensical concept of feeling unfulfilled without children.

Does that not put our capacity to have sex at our own desire into a new light? As far as the human race is concerned (and it's only humans that have developed this level of controllability) the sexual act has developed from being merely the essential instinct for the survival of the species. Absolutely uniquely, human beings alone have the ability to *enjoy* having sex without its primordial need for procreation purposes, it means that we can enjoy sex for the pleasure that it provides, for the bonding or renewing of a couple's affinity and love, and for the intimate, singular binding of lifelong partnerships. To summarise the situation unambiguously, sex as such is no longer needed (or required) for the essential proliferation and survival of the human species as it was historically. It is as a direct result of our advancing intelligence that we slowly progressed through using sex for both reproductive purposes and entertainment value, until it has become primarily for the joy of loving.

But it is this same intelligence that now has another even more essential function. With the impending overpopulation/under-resourced crisis then, for humanity's sake, our powers of logical reasoning must be brought into action. Sex for reproduction in a world which has more people than it can accommodate is simply mindless. Some might argue that more *can*_be provided-for, but look at the hungry around the world, work out the perversity of the doubling masses and face the facts of the issue. It is common sense to acknowledge that the *principle* purpose for sex is for pleasure and bonding partners: in other words, making love.

Surely that isn't too harsh a situation to live with, but is there any choice?

Disagreeable, distressing, problematic – perhaps, but only if the existing situation and its vital treatment are not confronted as a matter of urgency. Taking any route whereby reproduction is reduced to an absolute minimum, however that is achieved, is not only the course of sheer common sense, but the *only* path along which preservation of our race can continue. If you work it out, there simply is no possible way we can continue along this crazy and suicidal doubling-every-few-decades path. If we try to evade the issue by pretending it doesn't exist or is of no importance, in the immature belief that something will come along and it will be alright, then the inevitable result is the failure of society and the rule of anarchy. When people get hungry and all relied-on domestic commodities are cut off, then anger and the 'scapegoat' attitude clicks in and it ultimately becomes a case of survival of the fittest. That, of course, will only apply if the nuclear factor has no impact on the outcome and with the Valhalla or Armageddon cultures' nuclear potential, there's not much chance of that! A frightful outlook indeed, but its awfulness doesn't make it any less authentic. It's all there to be seen, but in order to see what's there, one's eyes have to be open, not inanely shut!

To summarise, we'll either have to recognise the situation as it is and exercise our human ability to limit population numbers to those which are sustainable within our means, or else the laws of nature will execute the task for us. Can anything be more clear and undeniable than that?

Chapter 8

Just Why There's "None So Blind..."

An insight into the mindset behind our reluctance to concede the problem

This is a contentious and far-reaching subject, up against an abundance of people who prefer not to know about it and are blindly dismissive. Unless the observations and subsequent conclusions offered in this book are a load of rubbish without any realistic foundation or substance whatsoever, the coming disaster cannot be avoided. So, is this just unsubstantiated waffle? If not, we've got big trouble!

No matter how much you might dislike the contents of this book, no matter how some might like to contemptuously pretend that they cannot relate to the forecast Armageddon by dismissively stating that they do not believe the evidence of presented observations, and that being without reams of statistics and quotations then the observations and opinions cannot be valid, then it is suggested that this reluctance is nothing more than wilful blindness; reluctance to see that which is not wanted to be seen. How childish is that?

Strident and alarmist it might be, uncomfortable reading it certainly is, but surely the momentousness of the subject-matter justifies a little fortitude. See if you still think it's been overemphasised when you get to the last page. We are in serious trouble. Not in a few generations' time, but now. But it seems that hardly anyone is interested, aware enough, (or, perhaps, brave enough?) to stand up and make an issue of it! To bang the wake-up drum noisily and conspicuously enough so that it cannot be ignored any longer, so that we get off our self-satisfied, complacent backsides and at least acknowledge the situation. Stop pretending that global overpopulation isn't a grave problem and start to see that the authorities that are in a position to do something about it. That is the problem, and the title of this book says it all. We don't want to see it, so we turn a blind eye to it! But why? Why won't we open our eyes to the coming crisis? Can't we see the diminishing resources conundrum? Can't we work out that a multiplying populace needs *more* resources, and that they're running out? Are we really so short-sighted that we can't grasp the immediacy and the global extent of the population predicament? Are we actually so blind to the imminent impasse that we genuinely can't see it coming, or do we somehow believe that two absolutely irreconcilable conditions such as these can somehow co-exist? Many questions, but they all confirm one supposition, and that will probably be obvious to the reader by now.

In addition to this conjecture, let us examine the way in which our elected governmental representatives (who are supposed – and paid – to look after our interests and welfare) are 'failing to see' the approaching disaster. Despite their fiddling of the unemployment statistics and other chicanery in order to conceal the growing overpopulation dilemma, whilst very carefully avoiding any mention of it, for how long can they keep up the pretence that they're not aware about the politically-unavoidable and deteriorating predicaments? Surely it is their duty to come clean and make it all publicly known before it blows up underneath us? It is only by recognition and with plans for some sort of preparatory action that we can even hope to prepare for the coming crisis. But no; our trusted representatives prefer to keep their heads down, pretend that everything in the garden's lovely and carry on with their statistics fiddling to convince us that it is. All the while they magnanimously present us with their self-compiled, self-aggrandising comfort images. A few politicians might point to the reducing level of their borrowing whilst having to apply their "stringency measures" while others try to make an issue of the alleged ensuing hardship. It is all a political charade, as a result of their long-overdue recognition of the fact that the era of courting the electorate by scrounging immense loans is over. Stringencies are merely the tip of an immense iceberg, testing the water in preparation for the presentation of some uncomfortable facts to an unpredictable electorate! If it all hits the fan in another part of the world first, then our officials will have to answer nasty questions, making it clear that they already knew of the coming crisis and that there is much worse to come! That's what democratic politics is all about: keeping your voters on a comfortable cushion or getting voted out, walking a thin line between "telling them what they want to hear" and keeping quiet when there's something nasty around that you don't want known. Voters, though, aren't going to take very kindly to news of an impending population/financial crisis, never mind the measures to address it. Even if it hasn't deteriorated so far that it's beyond dealing with! So, isn't it an obvious case of keeping schtoom, or getting voted out? Wouldn't you do exactly the same?

But where does self-preservation end and a sense of what's right and wrong begin?

Clearly, as far as our governmental representatives are concerned, if they are able to avoid breaking bad news then they will. But, if the bad news becomes worse with every passing day it's not attended to, ultimately becoming so bad that it's uncontainable, then the avoidance of breaking the news will become no more than apologetic excuses at best. Sensationalistic? Just think about it all: the possible breakdown of the society we all depend upon. If the over-riding human instinct of self-preservation is unleashed in the areas or communities that cannot support or control disruption, imagine the consequences! "More to be supported than we can support" is a formula for disaster, intensified by those who sense that the issue is probably terminal and resort to a primitive 'opportunistic greed' culture, as increasingly seen on our TV screens.

Viewing the situation from the political aspect, we can see that our government cannot be other than aware of the coming crisis and its inevitability. This is confirmed by the convoluted methods undertaken to conceal the cause of the problem by manipulation of the unemployment/overpopulation statistics, why the politicians (being human) prefer to keep their electorate's complacency (and their jobs) by hiding the mathematical inevitability of the crisis, and how, by evading the issue, they are <u>knowingly</u> allowing it to worsen with the passage of time. Not only that, but we can also see the difficult political balance between "....the sense of what's right and wrong...." and that of self-preservation; not an easy one to criticise?

Back to the 'buck-passing' sleight-of-hand, where a problem that can be discreetly postponed by one party will be left for an incoming party to inherit. In these days of growing electorate unrest and consequential changes, this is an inviting tactic to employ. Particularly if recognition of the postponed problem will almost certainly end in social breakdown one way or another.

But is the problem unanswerable?

Let's look at the available options. First, there are no defensive measures being taken. Leaving things as they are, without any control, means that sooner or later there will be insufficient food, water and power, leading to mass deaths by starvation or from violent repercussions as a result of this. Simply unthinkable! Second, there's the controlled birth restraint option. This would be impossible to enforce in democratic societies and also wide-open to self-enhancing exploitation by certain already-overcrowded domains using their untouchable religious arguments. Simply unsustainable!

If voluntary birth control is out, that just leaves the compulsory restriction option. Quite simply, it's essential, or the result will be unthinkable. So, *is* it unsolvable?

The facts in this book are either well known and generally accepted, or they are realities that can easily be confirmed. As are the particulars, assertions and predicted consequences about the *status quo* and the path we are following that some are so reluctant to recognise. Basic mathematics and common sense will positively and irrefutably assert the authenticity of this uncomfortable but undeniable impasse. Like gangrene, the longer that it's left unattended to fester, the more vital and perilous the surgical treatment will become. A distasteful analogy, maybe, but the gravity of the condition and its lack of recognition demand shock tactics.

Compulsory birth control! How democratic is that? And how many readers will be tempted to dismiss the idea as unacceptable? But the reader might find the following to be pertinent.

There is a sensitive issue in certain religions whose traditions ban any form of birth control. But for control measures to work, everybody must comply with the restrictions. No special cases or exemptions, especially if, as suggested, there are no sound or intelligent arguments that are able to pragmatically justify any such vindication. Is it not coincidence that in ancient history when religions were new and had every reason to exploit any method available to expand their proportion of the community these dictates were implemented? As a direct result of the dictates being faithfully followed, then that particular sect of the population gains numerically with progressively more and more believers being added to their ever more fervent flock? In effect, it's a form of auto-enlargement; a principle that any business would like to be able to emulate.

Returning to compulsory birth control, it must be clear that for this to succeed it has to be rigidly applied by all, not just by atheists. But is it even possible that birth control on a compulsory basis can be introduced on a global scale? Is it likely that all of those problematic religious sects can be persuaded to revise their decrees and convince their followers to comply? It might take a disaster or two first.

The reason for broaching the condition at this point is that it is more than likely the less-than-aware or the immovably-disciplined readers will have dumped it before now as being "unreadably disagreeable" without bothering to ask themselves why it should be so. Not wishing to appear immodest, however, it is humbly suggested that they might well ruefully recall this rejection in a few years' time when the "unthinkable" starts to unfold! Such dismissal, of course, is anyone's prerogative but, and again it is asked, is there ANY part of this manuscript that is untrue? Has it made any claims or statements that cannot be confirmed, or that have no sound or logical reasoning to support them? More to the point, and however distasteful some of the contents may be to some, after they have been read and (importantly) understood then, supposing that the predictions that are about to be forwarded as a reasoned interpretation of these contents can be accepted as being based upon well-founded logic and common sense (or even if they cannot be absolutely ruled-out from being a genuine possibility), then wouldn't it be a blindly and possibly irresponsible act not to at least check these allegations so that, if found to be sound and the threat to be real, then it's presence can be indicated and awareness be broadcast? Taking it further, would it not be a matter of moral and social duty to warn as many who will listen, however distressed they might be? The evidence is there but, in order to see it, one's eyes need be open.

Chapter 9

Brass Tacks Time

The only way to address overpopulation is reproduction control

The biggest problem is that of balancing the reader's interest against the human instinct to avoid news that evokes psychological unease. On the other hand, if the message that this book conveys really makes its point and is taken seriously, it could spark the fire of productive awareness. However, the unwelcome subjects and the distress factor means that the issues must be described in such a way as to provide convincing evidence to support and validate difficult contentions. In addition to that, it has to be presented as relatively old news for readers who might already be partly aware of the problems and inherent dangers. Perhaps they might have preferred not to discuss their suspicions and unease, or haven't fully probed the issues to realise the horrific potential outcome. In other words, the issue might have been shelved for comfort.

There are also those who will have realised the approach of the coming impasse but have found it to be less disturbing either to actively dismiss or to subliminally deny the daunting premise. Then there are those who are confident that, however huge, the problem will resolve itself, perhaps through some form of celestial intervention…

That should cover the range of awareness that this composition is tailored for but I suggest that there is one barrier common to all readers with a religious background. That is the next subject to be examined with more depth. Like any problem, before anything can be done about it, it has first to be recognised as a problem. It might sound a little patronising but, as in the case of patients with paranoia or compulsive fixations, the biggest step towards achieving recovery is gaining the patient's recognition that there is anything unnatural in their way of life. The same applies to the effects of ingrained beliefs.

This is all a reflection on what a wonderful mechanism the brain is. For example, just think how multi-directional the brain's receptive aptitude is during our formative years. So many lifelong disciplines are absorbed without either the need or the ability to question them, and they stay embedded in our psyche, usually for life. "Formative years" are just that. When we don't have a very high I.Q. but, as a response to our evolutionary patterning, we are programmed to take on board and absorb virtually everything that is obliquely noticed, or is told or demonstrated to us by our parents and teachers. We take in all of this character-forming knowledge and guidance *without in any way questioning its authenticity or rationality*. Having had it all firmly imprinted, it usually takes a lot of convincing to change a person's way of thinking.

That brings us to the second of the problems which need to be brought into perspective, and this is somewhat more compound.

It is our acceptance (or, more specifically, our unwillingness to concede) that we might have been misinformed, however unintentionally, that is at the core of the dilemma. I could point out that innovation and the constructive revision of viewpoints, beliefs, ways of thinking and so on, really represent nothing more sinister than the basic principles of education and enlightenment. But there is more to the voluntary and comfortable unblocking of deep-rooted and possibly outdated opinions than that. It is a human foible to dismiss anything which contradicts or challenges our entrenched understandings. In the light of life's experience, not many will dispute this. When an alternative viewpoint puts a different light on a subject that we have been brought up to believe is sacred and unarguable, then it is even more readily-dismissible!

However, as these contemporary convictions happen to be based or founded upon both confirmable observations and logical deductions rather than upon aged hypotheses based on absolutely un-provable (and often unbelievable) stories, there should not be many who wouldn't welcome them as rational revisions.

Even more disagreeable to the traditionalist's mind is any suggestion that such complacency and stubborn blindness might actually present an imminent threat to humanity! So you see what an immense uphill struggle we face.

Despite the psychological barriers, it is the sheer magnitude of the quandary which has to be carefully explained. It is a challenge that cannot be left in the vague hope that others just might pick it up. It must be shouted from the balconies so that anyone with principles might pick up the cause, bang their drum and hope that others will bang their bigger ones!

Overpopulation! If it can be accepted that this is not merely a problem, but one that's size and significance is being covertly concealed as detailed earlier, then it will be understood why it is so necessary to have an in-depth and unambiguous analysis of the issue, so that the possibility of urgent constraint can be considered.

The first thing that has to be faced is the obvious but untalked about fact that sex is the root of the dilemma. It also presents, for several reasons, the biggest obstacle that this composition has to contend with.

It is a very sensitive subject, so let's start the observation this way. Primarily, of course, it has to be acknowledged that some drastic and fundamental changes in the basic motivating force that stimulates both the male and female pursuance of sexual intercourse will have to be considered. No longer is (directly or subliminally, and at least in the majority of associations) reproduction the prime objective of sexual intercourse. Parenthood, perhaps, but not reproduction or contributing to the species. Continuance of the human race does not have any further place in our circumstances, and this is a logical fact that we dismiss at our peril. Humanity, the single life-form in a position to discerningly control both the purpose and the outcome of sex, has reached an acutely pivotal stage in its evolution. We have arrived at the barrier of unlimited proliferation's practicality, where the original purpose of its drive has now reversed. Rather than being essential to the species' continuance, it has now actually become a serious threat to our very existence. If that sounds outrageous, it will be fully explained in due course.

Far from just limiting our own numbers to maintain the current population level, we who are able and educated enough to exercise constraint have to take into account the effect of those who can't or won't and the effect of diminishing resources! The resources are going to run out whatever we do!

Perhaps the previous paragraphs have put a dreadful situation into perspective for the sceptical reader? The size of the issue, its possible solution and its psychological impact and eventual acceptance, have been presented for proper deliberation, rather than being kept out of sight by those who should know better!

The cognitive and psychological barriers have been tentatively mentioned and their salience predicted, and the need for reassessment of our conscious and subliminal sex-drive has been examined. We have put into a rational perspective how the conditioned-in need for sex has gradually changed from the primitive, purposeless urge and it's simple necessity for our basic survival, to planned' reproduction. This is concurrent with the gradual creation and exploitation of the mutual pleasure factor. So now, with the delicate subject broached and laid out before us, we're in a position to look at all these issues a lot more subjectively.

Chapter 10

Back To Our Origins

Balancing the fundamental purpose of reproduction against a changed situation

Before approaching more intimate subjects, it has to be respectfully pointed out that the entire purpose of this book is to put some out of date ideas into a modern perspective in order that fresh and, importantly, realistic deliberation can be applied, These ideas and deliberations appertain to the complex and analogous psychological development of sex.

Our intelligence slowly developed and, with it, the unemotional 'sex act' evolved into "making love" as the partnership culture came into being. This change of emphasis is of crucial importance for, as the primitive but naturally crude sexual urge slowly became one of purposeful reproduction, it also occasioned a new impulse which was pivotal in our species' distinctive progress. One which ensued alongside and logically as a consequence of the "partnership culture", automatically evolving and, as defined by evolution itself and as a matter of natural course, strengthened by each generation's genetic composition.

This, of course, is the sensual pleasure factor! Now, some might not like this, but it's a 100%-essential ingredient in the line of reasoning upon which this part of the book depends. It works like this: as human intelligence developed and deductive rationalisation grew to become progressively more influential in mankind's life, he found that the relative security of being able to cohabit with one mate, of staying with his own offspring and of balancing a home/food-preparing/hunting-gathering delegation-pattern or routine with just one partner. Slowly, but almost automatically, the comfort and reliability of this one-to-one association progressed into communities becoming monogamist. And so the emotion that we know as love evolved. It might sound a bit obvious, but I'm getting to the point.

Loving couples dedicated to each others' welfare and pleasure, with sex as it would have been in those early times, probably little more emotionally gratifying than that which all the other animals experience, then the act of having sexual intercourse would have been more for shared intimacy than for the pleasure that we are familiar with. That's where evolution comes in – whatever the degree of enjoyment that did manifest itself, then those couples who achieved more in the way of pleasure from the physical act than those who didn't would have had more reason for, and hence more, sexual activity than those who didn't. As a direct result of this, their more sexually-responsive genes would have been passed on to their (naturally more-numerous) offspring. Consequentially, through the successive generations, the less-active, less-responsive gene-lines died out, and the more-intense, orgasmic experience that is (also as a result) unique to the human species would have evolved, slowly but, as above, inevitably intensifying into today's level of ecstasy as it did so. That is nothing more than simple, basic evolution!

In short, it is a perfectly natural, self-escalating process. Now, is not that the application of fundamental logic, and does this not explain quite feasibly and understandably why the sex act is of virtually no interest to some creatures when "outside the mating season", or even to others such as monkeys and dogs that are not seasonally-limited, but that clearly don't get any more pleasure out of it than that of their programmed-in "fulfilment-factor"? It also explains how precise "in-season" times were able to evolve, that sex to everything other than human beings is nothing more than a purely programmed-in function, and why this ingrained or implanted sex act is an automatic act about as satisfying to the animals as a sneeze!

Back to the three levels of sexual inducement. First, there's the universal, instinctive, usually year-cyclical impulse that is quite powerful enough without any need for a sensual 'reward' or gratification to trigger it. Second, there's the intelligence contingent and exclusively human, procreation motivation which, as suggested, would have originally been naturally-induced as above, but also had the additional attraction of self- and species-preservation to promote it. Third, there is the pleasure-generated and very specifically human orgasmic inducement that evolved from the second-level of inducement, evolving along a curve of "better-sensation-response/more-reason-for-sex/higher-offspring-output/more-active-gene-inheritance/even-better-sensation." As a consequence, we are the only, yes, animals that have, as a result of our intelligence, evolved our own orgasmic 'reward' system. But there is an important punch-line which warrants all this preamble. Human beings, whilst benefiting from our advanced intelligence, have also reached a level of ecstasy that is, in some cases, so powerful as to be more than a person is able to control. Right from the very first instance, reproduction has been an absolutely automatic urge. There was no planning or enticing strategy; it was like eating, a response to a need. It is just such an instinctive impulse which has been the singular agency for life on Earth and evolution. We cannot say for how many millions of years, but there is one thing we can be sure about. Right through our development from cellular life to today's level of advanced intellectual capacity, the reproduction impulse has been strong enough to become a major orientation for all life on Earth. Now, to put a lot of smugness into context: why is it that so many people like to think that this conditioning is likely to disappear overnight? The inbuilt urge to breed-without-motive has its roots deep in the subconscious mind. This trait is evidenced by the fact that its effect is shown quite positively in a "natural human reluctance" to even consider population control despite the logical outcome of its repudiation.

So, if the 'first level' is, in effect, nothing more than primitive inducement at a subliminal plane and this subconscious desire is revealed as such when exposed to logical study then this investigation shows that this primal programming is both based on outdated conditions and is a dangerous course to follow. It can then be put into perspective and dismissed. The same applies to the second level of inducement: the intelligence-conditional, procreation-motivated drive that, by definition, has to be even more readily viewed and dismissed. The third and purely pleasure-inspired reason for having sexual intercourse has, again by definition, to be optional.

With the first two inducements argued from a new, realistic viewpoint, then only the third is of any relevance. That means that to the aware mind, sexual intercourse need have no purpose other than that of having, and giving, the ultimate sensual pleasure. Procreation, now, is nothing more than an option that can, and needs to be, strictly controlled, or else!

This chapter has been particularly difficult to compose in a form that both confronts a principle that the majority regard as more of a right than an objective instinct. It also has to be sure that its structure carefully and sensitively explains some elementary principles from a completely new but elucidated aspect. These rationalised, logical views (as opposed to the stock, unquestioned ones) aim to put the entire issue of population into a sensible perspective without alienating traditionalists. In order to underline our unique, self-generated capacity to use sex for purposes other than reproduction, there is one other factor which needs to be considered. Other creatures are also capable of pursuing sex for pleasure and as such our "optional intercourse" prerogative also applies to them. However, this presumption needs to be seen from a more realistic viewpoint. The reason for emphasising this apparently-unimportant point will become clear later, but first it needs to be proved. Apart from the males of many creatures quite clearly being impotent and not even interested in sexual activity in out-of-season times or if, like monkeys and dogs, they do copulate but seemingly with little, if any, pleasure (especially in the eye-watering case of dogs), is this not the case of being the undeniable evidence of the power of that deeply-implanted driving- force behind the imprinted compulsion? Even when animals and birds are "on heat", the sex act is never seen to be warmly and embracingly enjoyed by participating pairs and it's usually, if not always, a case of 'the quicker, the better'! Enjoyment, pleasure, quite obviously no, and so it can only be as a response to the powerful, inherent compulsion that has been inherent since life began. It is evident, then, that it applies to all creatures other than us! Scents, seasonal urges, lunar activity and so on, all of these amount to evidence that the unarguably-essential and necessarily powerful motivations for sex, and hence procreation, is nothing more discretionary, and nothing less than subliminal programming, in any form of life other than human beings.

But the point of the above observation is this: before the time that our evolving mental capacity and level of evolution was sufficient to provide the earliest vestige of an orgasmic reward to make sex something to look forward to and plan for, we too, no less than all the other creatures, absolutely depended upon our sexual compulsions being switched on by purely instinctive, inbuilt programming. Had this not been the case, we would not have reproduced and the species would have died out. However, we had that inbuilt instinct, were imprinted with that impulse, and there's no reason on Earth to assume that it doesn't still apply. Just look at the discomfort that many will sense when reading this. Why should it be unsettling? Because it goes against all that's been imprinted for as long as life existed, and this life-preserving level of subconscious programming doesn't just disappear overnight!

If you dispute this still, think about how many people you've spoken to who aren't as interested in having sex, but "put up with it" as a way of having a child? There are quite a few who "suffer the violations" of sex for this purpose which is precisely what we were inherently programmed to do. No doubt some might recoil at the idea of our being, conditioned into responding to such instinctive pressure? It could be, perhaps, that they feel more comfortable thinking that human beings are above being programmed in the way that animals are. Even then?

However, neither wishing to alienate anyone or to spend a lot of precious reading or writing time in contesting this viewpoint, I merely ask why it is that any such pre-programming or pre-birth conditioning should not apply to primitive man whilst all the rest of nature can be seen to rely

100% on this subliminal conditioning for their survival. Why, also, should it be in any way less efficient (or essential) than its modern replacement, today's customary "facts of life" routine? Also, before we were able to use the power of speech, would not such programming have been no less essential for our own very survival as a species and, furthermore, as for the "Above being imprinted in the same way as animals" snub, are we not animals, then?

The problem is that from our modern, comfortably provisioned position, it's all too easy to underestimate the sheer strength and primal influence of subliminal, ingrained conditioning, and how we can be absolutely unaware of the influence it has over so many aspects of life. Even with all our wonderful modern technology and knowledge, we can only hazard a guess at how instinct succeeds in timing and navigating inestimable numbers of fish, birds, insects and mammals for often many thousands of miles, with utterly impeccable timing through any variety of changing atmospheric or geological conditions, all in order to reach a sometimes inch-perfect destination-point. Not only the annual migrations, but this precision also applies to the fixed-period or meteorologically-stimulated spell, sometimes decades-long, that some creatures comply with for their own breeding programmes. All this without any help from maps, Satnavs, notes or verbal instructions, and very often without even their parents to show them the way! How do they do it? We cannot be sure, but we can be certain that whatever it is that drives these prodigious feats, it's always motivated by and for the breeding compulsion, and that is overwhelming evidence of the force that can overcome all hazards. In other words, it is proliferation that motivates life.

That is a measure of how powerful it is, how universal, how subliminal and irresistible. That is the force that applies no less categorically to us. So, with such an immense level of influence, control and pressure on such an immense proportion of the world's creatures in one way or another, the purpose of this descriptive page or two is to illustrate just how unbelievably powerful this particular force is.

Not only from the emigrational aspect, this force also applies to some fixed-location creatures whose visual displays, odour-release, rousing-calls and other such stimuli, are induced by season, specific days, lunar positions, tidal conditions and so on. There are so many often life-imperilling male and female inducements/arousal antics, each one designed to excite, but inevitably they are species-wide and very often performed without instruction or demonstration by the parent.

So, if all the other creatures that exist on Earth are subjected to and comply with this colossal and inexorable force (the programming of which both naturally and crucially evolved, it must be remembered, from the very dawn of life, growing stronger as the less-ingrained and weaker gene-lines died away), then how could it be even remotely credible to think that human beings would not have evolved under that same level of life-imprinting conditioning? Accordingly, and logically, how could such a degree of intensity *not* be a part of the human psyche?

Maybe these fundamental observations and the subsequent conclusions are still a little difficult to accept but, surely the simple logic of humans evolving the described development of sex-at-will or for pleasure only can't be unlikely? After all, over many, many generations, those who participate in sexual activity and fornicate more frequently, whether it be because they felt the programmed need or whether they wanted offspring, whether they enjoyed the intimacy with their partners or whether gratification from the developing orgasmic 'reward' made it worthwhile, then it meant that sex was more frequent; there were more offspring as a result; the offspring were all more than likely to carry the sexually-active gene; and so would their more-numerous families. Meanwhile, the less-active gene would die out. This is an unarguably logical scenario which explains the magnetism of sex.

The point of this section is to show that we can control or refocus our sexual activity, and that the emotions appertaining to such a basic change can be quite feasible. So, this is where the composition takes on a more amenable aspect.

Chapter 11

Recognising the Capabilities Evolution has Provided

A few examples of how we can utilise and control our instinctive functions

After the long-winded but hopefully adequate reappraisal of our attitude to sex, if it can be accepted that inbuilt conditioning played an essential part in our development, and conceded that the sexual impulse is adapted as a direct result of our evolving gene-lines, then it shouldn't be too difficult to take the next logical step in our quest to refocus our sexual desire. Away, that is, from the primitive purpose of reproduction.

If you think about it dispassionately, it is only a matter of recognising the conformist, traditional attitude for what it is in order to bring it under control, just as we have done before with fire, for example. As with so many other examples, the first knee-jerk reaction was to get away from fire as quickly as possible, as demonstrated by all other animals. Now, before revising our way of thinking we'd have always done just that, but once we'd reached a level of intellect that allowed us to control this faculty, and learnt to constrain our inbuilt fear of it, the harnessing of fire became an absolutely essential part of our everyday life. Quite clearly there is a vestigial degree of respect for it, but nowadays we couldn't do without it. There's another example that illustrates how objective attitude change altered our lives: how we curbed an instinct that evolution had programmed into us, transposing it to subdue and utilise the threat of certain animals for our own benefit. It is only a matter of a millennia or two ago that packs of wolves and other canine species hunted and preyed on our ancestors as one of their natural sources of food, presenting a considerable threat to our communities. Since then, we have completely reversed this danger, learning to domesticate and interbreed their derivatives. Dogs are now known as "man's best friend". Fortuitous attitude change!

There are instances which might appear superfluous now, but none the less I underline the reasons for showing these examples. For example, there are numerous cases of dangerous and often enormous animals to which our involuntary auto-recoil reaction is now held in check. The purpose of calling your attention to them is to illustrate how, in history, and as our intelligence and manipulative abilities evolved, we have proved ourselves to be quite capable of acknowledging, then seriously re-evaluating and controlling our natural reactions, inborn fears, fixations and obsessions. However, that is precisely the reason that these examples are being brought into focus, to illustrate how our new perceptiveness gives us an awareness that not everybody is able to appreciate. In other words, these are examples that provide absolutely positive proof of how we are capable of recognising evolved-in reactions for what they are. Simply by understanding and changing our attitude, we can exploit these for our own benefit.

The purpose of this preamble is to demonstrate how this unconscious compulsion to proliferate can be put into the proper survival-perspective and then be intelligently managed. We are now perceptive enough to rethink our outdated attitudes to sex and its purpose. In fact, the original attitude to sex and its purpose simply cannot continue to be utilised for indiscriminate procreation. There is clearly no room on the planet for this, and we do so at our peril! There's no choice about it, for our own sakes and that of our limited offspring, we have to change our way of thinking about sex and to utilise it for its unique way of sharing pleasure. Surely that cannot be a bad thing?

An exploitative viewpoint, could be, but that certainly doesn't make its speculations and conclusions less sound. The only real loss is the frightful penalty of overpopulation. Once again, it is a case of analysing some strategically concealed facts, and then viewing their salience in the light of new and life-critical evidence.

This book is significantly more subdued than the size and severity of the developing crisis really calls for, in order to treat possibly offensive issues with sensitivity. The matter of our being deluded by those in government needed to be called to attention and detailed before it would be believed! That might explain the so far fairly restrained level of writing. It is a case of applying psychology for discretionary reasons, but I hope that interest has overcome distaste. In the light of this, a little polite and preparatory explanation will be expedient before we venture on to the less-cushioned, more unambiguous section ahead.

My previous caution can be summarised as follows: the origins and the development of one or two traditional human 'understandings' have been surveyed in the light of their foundations and balanced against modern knowledge, which provides evidence for any conflicting allegations. The matter of the approaching disaster was put into a verifiable aspect with uncomfortable, security-prejudicing details. The constructive use of our intelligence has been suggested as being both the indirect cause of the coming crisis and the tool with which it will, sooner or later, have to be tackled. Overpopulation and its cause has been addressed, as has the way in which political cushioning has so far succeeded in hiding it.

Now that the context has been successfully presented without being casually dismissed as inconceivable, then we shall examine the details of the associated issues in much closer detail.,

The next few chapters might challenge certain beliefs and suppositions.

However, I hope to revealingly and constructively examine some issues that could inspire some serious reconsiderations.

To close this chapter: it has been shown that all isn't well in our world. There is a fundamental necessity to acknowledge and make some effort to address the approaching quandary. But the observations and conclusions within belong to the writer and, as such, are open to question and the reader's own confirmation. If these conjectures come to be accepted, I hope it will result in another's loudly banging the drum in order to open more eyes to the crisis.

Chapter 12

An Evolved Ability that must first be recognised as such

How instinctive reactions can quash common sense

I hope the previous chapters will have inspired the reader's adoption of the theory about our evolutionary self-programming and, perhaps, the way we have developed a subtle redirection of the motivations which arouse our basic desires and urges. Having opened the door to both self-management of our intrinsic conditioning and the urgency of activating this capacity, the next item on the agenda is how to refocus our desires and drives so we can prevent their becoming serious stumbling blocks. However, there is another obstacle in the way: a barrier which causes even the most resolute to men to completely forget their strategic principles of conquest, their intended composure and their important precautionary measures. This obstacle is adrenaline.

Adrenaline is the cause of many unanticipated situations. If it were not for the thrill, the spontaneity and the potent spur of this particular stimulant, then we might not have an overpopulation crisis!

We have to live with adrenaline, though and I am certain most of us would not want to be without it. So, in order that nothing physical or psychological is jeopardised, we have to take an objective look at adrenaline to see how it works and is protected.

So very often precautionary plans have been made, but it is the blinding intensity of those highly-charged, often unexpected and excitingly special occasions that makes these situations so vulnerable to mistakes, carelessness often expensively repercussive oversights.

I suggest that most of us can probably recall such a circumstance or two, especially in the bloom of youth. We might well have breathed a huge sigh of relief to later learn that we have "got away with it". As we all know, good luck cannot be relied on, particularly when it has a potentially life-changing impact.

It takes a great deal of self-control for a couple to resist ecstatic compulsions and stand back to ensure that contraceptive precautions have been taken. It is a distraction when any distraction is least welcome.

Such is the circumstance which applies most manifestly (and dangerously) in the impulsive vigour of youth. Sexual activity is at its height, with the new thrill of discovering all the different emotions and experiences, hedonistic urges are at their peak, and thoughts about the future are of fleeting account, if at all. Of course, this description does not necessarily apply to everybody, but certainly to the average person.

So, back to the potentially life-changing contingencies at this time of life. This is precisely the period when the possibility of conception is at its peak and the consequences of indiscretion are most likely to result in an "accident" which can have a fateful influence upon the biggest and most important part of two individuals' lives. This often also has a religious pretext.

Correlating the above reflection's influence on overpopulation requires a logical speculation; if adrenaline is both the main cause of life-disrupting "accidents" and something the majority of us would definitely not want to be without, then what is the answer to this conundrum? We need an answer which actually will ensure there is no chance of a lifelong commitment. We don't want to waste precious foreplay or loving time having to prepare for love-making. We also need to address the subliminal female fear of being 'left' with any problem. Such an answer would avoid apprehensions from either side about reliability of the contraceptive used. On the subject of contraceptives, family planning (or would, perhaps, the term "race saving" now be more appropriate?) can take many forms, from the somewhat desensitising but effective condom, the "Must not be forgotten" contraceptive pill, the morning after pill, to more intrusive but absolutely 100%-effective surgical procedures.

But family planning also applies to the all-important matter of self-management. One has to ask just how many potential parents are responsible and organised enough to make the effort to properly weigh all the many points at issue when they plan to take a step as life transforming as starting a family? For instance, the all-too-often ignored time factor: two or more decades of dedicated parental commitments and responsibility would lie ahead of them. That is a long period of devotion and obligation which must be shouldered whatever unseen circumstances arise. What about the incalculable direct and indirect monetary expenses and encumbrances – so many of these are absorbed without even thinking that they apply! What about more predictable worries involving behaviour and education, or "unexpected" interests and activities, obscure friendships and visits, employment apprehensions, Internet or similar anonymous contacts and indiscretions? These worries will particularly apply when the growing unemployment scenario means that there will be many more youngsters wandering about with absolutely nothing to occupy their active but disillusioned minds!

All of the above is not mere speculation, but an inevitable part of the future. Who would want to bring up a family into that sort of world? Just what would be the point? This is without thinking about the situation from a green point of view! There is also an issue from the perspective of the married couples: despite the usual parental obsession with diligently concealing their anxieties from others, they'll be quite aware that the above situations, and probably a lot others too, can overburden even the strongest partnership.

Whilst on the subject of parental obsessions, is it not virtually always the case when contentions such as those above are raised that strident objections like "Oh no, I just KNOW that my child would never even think of doing something like that!" come out of the woodwork? Are such declarations nothing more than complete and unqualified fantasy? Whatever the situation, there is absolutely no way that any parent can foresee the future, and love of one's child is no guarantee of their integrity. After all, with nothing more than one chance meeting at a pub, club or bus queue, or maybe at a football match or party can lead to a string of events that can utterly transform anyone's life, for better or worse. It's an irrefutable fact that nobody's child, however much loved, is immune from this fact of life.

It is a predictable unpredictability and an inescapable part of growing up through childhood, adolescence and single life. Unpleasant and distasteful situations and relationships can always arise and, like it or not, it's the parents who have to be the buffers.

Chapter 13

And There's More…

Just a few of the advantages gained from a child-free life

The diplomatically-suppressed features of parenthood mentioned in the previous chapter are far from being all the potential menaces. In addition to these and many other hazards, it must not be forgotten that problems, commitments and responsibilities don't just disappear overnight when the children grow up and leave the comfort and security that has been provided for them. On the contrary, the only real difference is that "out of parental care" means that they are away from parental observation and guidance, so unchecked and bigger mistakes can be made. But long-standing parental buffers still exist, and can be called upon (however deviously).

Another factor to be considered, particularly in view of the current economic climate, is the growing consequences of the restrictions having a family imposes on a couple's freedom, particularly the mobility and ability to change or seek employment and/or move house at will around the country or abroad.

In short, life without children is not just possible, but can offer a blissfully unfettered lifestyle which enables a couple to fully enjoy everything they might wish to, with freedom to relocate for work or any other reason.

However, I wouldn't mind betting that there are very few readers who feel completely at ease with this contention, and who would unhesitatingly concede the case for a child-free partnership. Who would openly recognise the immense advantages of such an enlightened revelation? Despite all the previous chapter's verifiable facts, who would accept the fundamentals of a child-free assertion without really knowing just why? That, of course, is the power of formative programming and social expectation. It can mould an entire life at a subliminal level and, unless this is explained, a person can be under an illusion for a lifetime. Instances of unthinking delusions will be described later.

So what are the reasons for making the above observations? Or, to put it into a logical context, the way that we can be moulded into beliefs from childhood without having the knowledge or incentive to question their validity. These often outdated misconceptions remain unquestioned because they provide a comfortable belief, or their religious aspect makes it 'disrespectful' to waver from the faith. They can remain as a life-governing influence.

The immense difficulty lies in tackling the tenacity of these imprinted contentions. A decision which might seem sound and logical, but happen to disagree with traditional convictions, then illogical programming kicks in and disrupts the application of common sense! Put another way, anticipating the reader's probable discomfort when reading the "child-free" suggestions above, is not this perfectly illogical, personal discomfort positive evidence in itself of just how subliminal conditioning and the resulting mind-set works? How the sheer, if implausible, strength of it can override clearly-proven logic and how it actively prevents intelligent decisions being made? So, if this conditioning isn't responsible for your unease, then what else could be?

To further this argument, in case there should still be some residual reluctance, the fact that tradition-challenging declarations of this nature cause any unease at all must provide clear verification of the alarming scale of this subliminal barrier. There are many who would be unable to explain *why* they feel disturbed by the child-free suggestion, but who would spontaneously and unthinkingly react to this unease with an instant dismissal of the idea.

This section might be repetitive and protracted, but it has a lot of inbuilt hostility to contend with. It takes a lot of interpretation and clarification to establish the case's authenticity. Remaining on the subject of causing unease, surely this symptom is itself demonstration of both the proof of its existence, and also the potency and stubbornness of outdated and logically unsound fixations? In addition, the evidence of these indications shows how essential it is to clear the mind of these symptoms.

It takes an uninhibited and unusually open-minded person to openly challenge all the indoctrinations of a lifetime. This particularly applies if that person happens to be a parent who has already fed the patterning disciplines of "dollies for little girls" and "when you grow up and are a father yourself" into the trusting and receptive mind of their own child.

If this person were to challenge all of their own indoctrinations, such mind-clearing would obviously involve countermanding all of the previous persuasions and expectations they fed to their child, putting these into a completely new perspective for them. Open admission of giving the wrong guidance is not easy for a parent, or anyone. It is difficult to openly contradict long-ingrained beliefs and replace them with full acceptance of logically perceived principles. Thus, all the more credit to a person with the courage and integrity to concede and make known their own awareness!

I hope that sufficient evidence has been given to prove that none of my observations are unethical or prejudiced. Any trepidation to voice acceptance is revealing: that symptom is a profoundly clear and unarguable confirmation of the extent of subconsciously ingrained assumptions that should be left for the individual to accept. Anything else is just indoctrination.

Is this a hard pill to swallow? Let me clarify further. Is it not a prerequisite for parents (who undertake a biological obligation to bring up a child to the best of their ability and knowledge) to provide moral guidance during the child's vulnerable, formative years? Is it not also a fact that some of this knowledge is adamantly stated to be true? As such, to question it is "wrong" or a "sin". Other customs and habits are also passed on by inference and consequential presumption.

This applies specifically to religious and progenitive disciplines.

In the event of this information's being recognised as undependable or even fictitious, are people who practice it not failing to meet, or even abusing one of the main responsibilities of parenthood? I refer to demonstrating by example not to take the uncorroborated view of others as being beyond question and avoiding any personal humiliation by failing to admit the passing on of inaccurate or misleading guidelines. Are you still apprehensive about the principle of blindly accepting traditional beliefs and the ethics of passing them on? To put it frankly, it is a case of brainwashing. There is no avoiding that allegation: this sort of implanting and entrenchment of growingly less-credible stories and suppositions, is precisely that. I mean the things children are fed by well-meaning parents, relatives, school-teachers, church officials and so on, in the years before they are old and worldly enough to make up their minds for themselves. The description may be distasteful, but can you dispute its accuracy? In our childhood we are by nature unquestioningly open and receptive. As such, we are coerced into believing things that our trusted (and also brainwashed) seniors follow. We have no choice.

When we are old enough to weigh up the facts we should be advised that "these are stories that we might believe in, however less than credible they might be", followed by the common-sense conditional "but whether you also choose to believe them or would prefer to follow your own thoughts on the subject is for you to decide, not us!" This might sound a little unlikely, but wouldn't it be nice to be told as a child that the choice of which, if any, faith we might wish to follow and, how we would like to programme our own lives, is not for our parents to decide. <u>It should be our own decision,</u> but in the light of what we've found out about life when we know enough to make that choice! Now, isn't that well-reasoned logic?

This hypothetical situation where young children are not subjected to the application of parental belief or persuasion, but are allowed the freedom to make up their own minds about religious matters in their own time and in the light of their own life-experiences might seem unnecessarily protracted, but there is a fundamental reason for this.

In fact, the next few chapters take on an illustrative, biographical aspect. The above situation, with no religious pressure during the formative years, applied to me as a child. This is a situation which few can claim to have made available to them, but it provided me with the and uniquely unconstrained potential to see the world and its psychology in a light far removed from the average. The purpose of this background will become clear in due course.

In view of the confrontational nature of this chapter, perhaps it might be rational to summarise it subjectively. It challenges a discipline normally assumed to be irrefutable. But that begs the question of <u>who</u> says it is, and under what jurisdiction? If it is a case of indoctrination by those who have already been indoctrinated then the validity of the discipline collapses under its own lack of credibility. Why, then, should it still retain the capacity to kindle those discomfiting reactions? That's how formative years teachings work. It's a direct result of our aeons of evolution that we've developed the naturally-productive practice of copying and absorbing everything that is fed to us at that time in our lives. This formative period covers the time when we have neither the intelligence nor the need to think for ourselves, through to the time that our brains have developed sufficiently for independence. It is during these receptive years that "teachings" are implanted. They are further galvanised by prevalence and by not being subjected to any analysis. Their unassailability gains strength almost as an automatic process. We have only to observe or recall our own parent/child and teacher/pupil instructional relationships to see for ourselves that this is true. The prodigious problem is that this "imprinting" (and it's formidable adhesion) has to be recognised for what it is before we can stand back and look at its basic credentials productively. Only then will we be in a position which allows proper <u>and impartial</u> questioning.

That is precisely what this chapter has tried to illustrate. Its purpose is to introduce a mature level of questioning scepticism into the ritualised beliefs and ways of life that the traditionalists of old followed. I have attempted to do this without causing too much angst whilst properly authenticating its basic validity, and to open eyes sensitively and gently.

Chapter 14

The Important Sexual Factor

There's one absolutely essential aspect which has to be properly addressed before the discussion of life without children is complete. That is the matter of sex – recreational sex, at least. For humans, the motivating drive for pursuing sexual activity has evolved away from breeding to pleasure.

In other words, a couple's natural sexual appetite can be reserved and practised merely for the mutual physical and psychological pleasure that it can provide. There is nothing wrong or immoral about that and there is nothing wrong in using that feature as an important element in establishing a pivotal argument.

Life without children has enormous advantages. When a couple live together, sexual activity is quite an important part of the compatibility-factor. A good sex life can, obviously, be substantially enhanced by an element of spontaneity, and a mutually-pleasurable sex life can be a significant feature in the quality of a couple's life together. All of this is forfeited with children on the scene. No doubt most parents can recall awkward interruptions and passion-killing concerns about the children walking in. There are also long periods of celibacy during pregnancy. The quality of the relationship can flourish without any of these inhibitions, which must surely be reflected in the partnership's solidarity. Partnerships with two people enjoying their uncomplicated lives together cannot be other than strengthened.

It is fortunate that we live in an age and environment where birth-control is both simple and usually positive. However, it is possible for the contraceptive pill to be forgotten, if that is the sole method relied upon. The most straightforward, safe and inexpensive method of birth-control is vasectomy. This is surprisingly advantageous from the value-for-money aspect.

The certainty achieved as a result this simple operation can only be an enormous psychological stimulus to both of the partners in a relationship where a child is not desired. Vasectomy provides absolute freedom from the latent possibility of an unplanned pregnancy.

The security that vasectomy provides is even more sensible outside an established relationship. A man who voluntarily chooses sterility makes a conscious contribution to address the overpopulation question, but also eliminates any fears about being caught out without condoms. In any case, the sensual advantages of being able to enjoy intercourse without a condom should not need any clarification.

The complex and wide-ranging nature of this particularly sensitive subject necessitates a thorough evaluation of as many facts and psychological considerations as possible. I must reiterate this vastly-underestimated outcome of vasectomy: the delight of completely spontaneous lovemaking without passion-killing considerations. A mere description cannot adequately convey the value of such spontaneity, even to long-established relationships. It's like the zest which fires up a new relationship. Predictability can bring about monotony, but the spontaneity factor can make an important difference.

In closing this section about the evident virtues of vasectomy, there is one particularly vacuous cliché which needs to be mentioned. I refer to reluctance to have a vasectomy based on anxieties about the loss of masculinity. This is grandiose twaddle. It is sheer ignorance to assume that vasectomy results in any kind of masculinity denial or sexual impairment. It probably camouflages nothing less than a childish timidity.

Unpalatable facts demand down to earth descriptions. For some, this might border on distasteful, but we have to embrace all levels of acceptance. There is no place for twee niceties and innuendos. It should also be remembered that there is the huge, self-suppressing psychological barrier which logical reality has to confront and overcome.

Let us not forget the emergence and vast enormity of the disaster Every piece of artillery which can be resorted to has to be used.

Chapter 15

A More In-depth Look at the Psychology that is Involved

Why should humans be different to all other animals on Earth?

I have discussed imprinting, but it is essential to recognise that although a belief may be 'imprinted', that does not mean it is indelibly so. In fact, if a new awareness of the conditions has already been accepted by the reader then, like so many other subliminal fixations, the very fact that the it has been recognised and acknowledged as such, means that 99% of the work has been done! Simple logic will do the rest!

The second prerequisite is to recognise that, as self-disciplined and independent individuals, we all have the capacity to use our unique strength of mind to restructure and actively replace the outdated motivation for sex with the updated one. We can substitute the idea of sex for the purpose of reproduction with the idea of sex for pleasure alone. The unique ability we have to utilise this asset is a result of our evolutionary advancement in conjunction with our intelligence and our contemporary knowledge.

The reason for returning to this subject is that it's a difficult concept to concede, especially when it contradicts lifelong understandings. Indeed, concerning the subject's credibility, it is the basic refocusing of sexual motivation that really is the crux of what this part of the book is about. Without compound explanations, interpretations and analyses, the sexual deductions might have been suspect and the conclusions readily dismissed. But it is nothing less than self interest that's at stake. Put another way, it is utterly essential that these observations are properly understood and accepted. Without our traditional instincts being shown to be programmed in, it would be quite pointless attempting to retune anyone from their ancient "automatic" mode to the logic-endorsed option.

This matter has already been alluded to, but as the following chapter tackles the differences between the basic and purely-instinctive urge-without-objective of sex as seen in other creatures, and our own evolved and self-motivated level of making love. As such, it delves into the very sensitive matter of our conscious, but newly-discovered, capacity to control its purpose.

For those already in full agreement with the previous submissions and suggestions, the next few paragraphs might be superfluous, but for those who might still not be quite ready for the reasoning that will verify the human race's unique capacity to direct or regulate the entire reason for having sexual intercourse, a little more animal/human differentiation might be needed.

As far as human beings are concerned it is the anticipation of sharing warmth and joy, intimacy and giving, that is just one aspect of the motivating incentives that initiates the "reproduction-sequence."

In the majority of cases it appears that the sexual union itself, the physical exhilaration of intimate union with the sensual and psychological uplifting boost constitutes the primary purpose for sexual intercourse. The reproduction-factor, if even considered at the time, usually takes a very secondary role in the activity.

Significantly, this is in direct contrast with the situation that applies to all other animals. Their stimuli are often triggered by one of many completely involuntary odours, colourings, appendages, etc. Crucially, these stimulating practices are always evolved such that the timing of the subsequent birth, egg-laying/hatching, spore or seed-release coincides with the seasonal supply of provisions so that the offspring survive. That is, of course, unless that particular species does not depend on seasonal nutrition, but that's the way evolution works.

In the light of all other creatures' sexual triggering, it could quite logically be argued that when animals mate, they are no more than <u>responding</u> to specific excitants and acting in the way that they are programmed to do. Then, with hereditarily-weaker or less-flamboyant strains automatically lessening through their producing less offspring through successive generations, the sex act and its linked relationship to the strength of this response to specific stimuli means that its intensity must increase through progressively more responsive generations. That, again, is how evolution works. Still, though, it is a purely instinctive impulse. Any plans about the proliferation of their species is the last thing on an animal's mind. As far as animals are concerned, whether sexual relief is an inducement or an automatic switch-on, the sexual act is definitely not consciously undertaken as a planned means to produce offspring! How can animals even be aware that the sex act results in future birth? Do they know or care about future species welfare? It is certain that their parents have no way of informing them about offspring-creation, even if they stayed around after their birth, and there are many species which don't.

If even the staunchest sceptic should still have any doubts about the evolutionary actuality of programming, its effect and the immeasurable strength of its subliminal control then surely these clear observations show that sex and mating is simply the result of a primal, elementary urge. This urge has grown and developed through the natural-selection/evolution principle into the psyche of all creatures. At this time, it's only mankind that this principle doesn't apply to, but it wasn't always so! More about that later.

As far as all other animals are concerned, evidence proves that neither are they aware that the sex act is part of the reproductive cycle nor are interested in procreation *per se*. Nor do animals have any reason to know that there is even a connection between the sex act and its consequences! This doesn't even take into account the probability of very limited memory-aptitude. Whatever level of insight, if any, is thought to exist, it must be obvious that it is definitely not the anticipated patter of tiny paws that prompts males to jump on females!

That brings me to a particularly pivotal stage in my argument. It is this: why should human beings think that we have evolved differently, or are dissimilar in our development, from all of other animals? Why should we alone have evolved an objective analysis of sex without having gone through a sequence of evolution where sex was a <u>motiveless</u> response to primitive compulsion? After all, we were reproducing quite successfully long before we were able to talk about it, let alone reach any reasoned conclusions or plans! Can the similarity between the comparative evolution of us and all of the other creatures on our planet be more indisputable?

In other words, it's a matter of sheer, basic common-sense logic to work out and accept the fact that we and all the other creatures on this planet evolved along similar evolutionary paths. These paths are branches which together constitute the tree of life. However, there is a more scientifically positive picture.

"Genetic Instruction" is the phrase used to describe the natural urge to propagate unthinkingly and without challenge. 'Instruction' implies that orders have been given. This conjecture is in need of updating to a rationalised, modern context. We now know that it is the result of our evolutionary development through countless generations and the consequent overwhelming of 'less-inclined' genes by the naturally more-prolific pro-breeding ones. But now the circumstances have completely reversed. This urge has now become an imminent threat to our very future. Fortunately the days when such 'instruction' had to be adhered to are now behind us. The urge can be easily redirected into its proper context as an obsolete directive. With time, it will become history, like the creation theory.

Chapter 16

It's All a Matter of Self-Control

Evolutionary development and how its roots need to be recognised

If you accept the previous observations about programming, the next stage is easy. Recognition that human procreation, whether planned or not, has to have resulted from our primordially complying to an automatic urge, then this means that the stage is set for the next step in our reasoning sequence.

It is a basic principle of evolution that we had the urge to engage in sex naturally instilled into our primitive brains. The gene lines which have sufficient motivation for this died out. So, like other surviving creatures, we developed through the generations a progressively stronger compulsion for sex. We had no knowledge of its purpose. We had no need to know about the connection between sex and the reproduction sequence. It was just a strong impulse that the future of the species happened to depend on. That is how the reproduction-sequence originated and how it developed through human evolution into the situation as it is now.

It developed from a primitive motiveless urge through intentional proliferation to the present reproduction/just-for-recreation options. However, the original necessity for sex for survival of the species is now completely transposed. Reproduction is no longer an essential function, but one that actually threatens human life on Earth if not drastically controlled. The primitive impulse which made sex and its consequences an asset has become a situation where sex itself has to be set apart from its natural purpose in order that it can remain practicable!

In other words, sexual intercourse will have to be reprioritised. We'll have to re-educate ourselves to use intercourse only for the purpose of pleasure. This might sound a little flippant, but there really is no alternative. When demand exceeds supply then people have to go without, whether the demand is for food, energy, water or anything upon which life might depend upon or be sustained by. If it's not there to sustain them, people die! However, that is only a part of the tragedy. There is a far more sinister aspect that kicks in when famine or other shortages reach a life-threatening magnitude. I refer to the way people are all too ready to exploit conditions with either strength or authority. When threatened with starvation or other life-threatening deprivation, there are many who would kill to live! The principle which applies here is 'the self before others', which defines the breakdown of law. It might be a dramatic picture, but it's an utterly rational illustration of social breakdown. If you want proof of this, then just look at the Middle East.

Mass and random reproduction is now no longer the essential formula for human survival. It has now snowballed into imminent and life-threatening peril. However, we should recognise this fundamentally decisive allegation, and then stand back impartially and confront all of those inbuilt or ingrained ritualistic fixations. Only then will we be ready to actively re-target the object of having sexual intercourse. Only when we manage to achieve this will our sleepwalk into disaster stand any chance of being turned aside.

The proposed, conscious self-control is set to be in direct conflict with traditional instincts. However, the often unrealised depth of the ingraining is an inevitable consequence of the almost incalculable number of former generations which have been feeding the chains of ongoing indoctrination. The validity of these old but stubborn complexes is being progressively eroded by constantly-improving intelligence. It won't be long before common sense puts sex into its new box.

This leads me to another observation, which is the gradual whittling-away of mental blocks as traditional beliefs and understandings are being discredited by discoveries and sound judgement. In other words, the stubborn blindness that has been endemic for so many decades is slowly melting away! Just as religion dominated the time before Darwin's revelations, all these uncorroborated stories and unexplainable directives will be put into their proper place and relegated to being just a part of our valuable history.

Post-Darwin, the inevitable conversion to enlightenment had, and still has, a lot of 'dead wood' to contend with. The stubborn blindness of so many will only very slowly decay away to insignificance.

In the meantime, the ritualised 'unlimited procreation' doctrine versus that of the 'innovation of essential control' is a conflict which, for every day that it is allowed to continue unresolved, results in the intensification of a predicament that is becoming less stoppable with the passage of time. It is the increase of demands and the decrease or exhausting of supplies. It is a conflict in which there will be no winners, only losers! Either we all put our ritualistic or compulsive 'need' multiply into its logical context, or we all go to the wall when society breaks down! Certainly, it is quite feasible that there might be some survivors, providing, of course, that the nuclear issue does not become involved. But it will only be the strongest and most ruthless who'll survive at the expense of the weak and ethical! That's humanity!

The human idiosyncrasy of pretending that a crisis doesn't exist is difficult to face, and so is the politicians feeding the gullible news they'd prefer to hear rather than the bad news that they need to hear to address it. Some might hope that the power of prayer will solve any problem, but remember the greedy who exploit any crisis in order to fleece the easily-deceivable, or those who exploit religious credibility for the implementation of terrorism! "Ethnic Cleansing", "Holy Wars": we have all heard these depictions and all know where these hats fit! It is this level of hypocrisy and thoughtlessness that I seek to put into focus.

But nobody wants to know about it. They just shut their eyes even tighter and shake their heads sympathetically. This is a classic case of the ever-decreasing circle, and we all know where that leads.

Like my suggestion about political concealment of overpopulation, it is equally feasible that the climate-change/global warming issue is being kept just as low-profile. Its extent and its threat-level might be being concealed for as long as possible. The answer why has already been covered: discontented electors don't vote for the carriers of bad news. Should the political system or the politicians be condemned?

Chapter 17

The Exposure and our Eventual Recognition of Overpopulation

The dangers we're not told about

Is it not perfectly understandable that the sheer magnitude of the overpopulation issue that prevents it from being confronted? In conjunction with its frightening inevitability and the terrible consequences of the backlash, this premonition represents the paradox where the depth of the conundrum and the fear of the reaction when it is finally broached eclipse honesty and the crisis' escalation.

It is quite possible, that the situation is not as serious and explosive as it appears to me. However, news reports show that concern is justified. It is not mere exaggeration to observe that oil-reservoirs and shale-gas are increasingly harder to reach and prejudicial to uncontaminated expanses of our planet, or that dams and deployment of fresh water upstream is depriving those downstream, or that more and more people are in famine conditions now that rainfall is no longer sufficient. None of that begins to take into account the effects of global warming.

These observations are not groundless, so why can't we acknowledge their presence? We seem blind to their unrestrained escalation, closing our eyes to the unavoidable calamities. We do nothing to confront and prepare for that which is ahead of us. So far, I have only touched upon the tip of a very sensitive iceberg.

I progress now to discussion of one of the most volatile issues in existence: sensitive, subjective and deeply entrenched. It is defended by its implied immunity from mention of anything unfavourable. To really add spice to the contention, its self-proclaimed insularity means that it can be the causal orchestrator of anything from city riots to mass-murders like the 9-11 atrocity. It can instruct any of its active extremists via "divine message" to perpetrate such foul exploits. So, why should these simple souls be prepared to die for these "causes"? There are two reasons. First, there is the basic exploitation of the fact these suicidal militants have absolutely nothing to lose by forfeiting their lives: no income, assets, or future. Second, any such activist will have been assured by his guru that he and his family will be rewarded for their 'bravery' in Valhalla or some other equally unlikely celestial paradise! This exploitative force is, of course, religion.

Religion: is there any subject which can raise emotions and reactions so intense, or that is so vigorously defended? It has so many different and contradictory viewpoints, doctrines and deductions. Dedicated followers of religion are all convinced that their belief is the only "true" belief. All others are dismissed as "heathens" or unenlightened. What about the huge and magnificent gold and jewel-bedecked properties into which hordes of impoverished worshippers humbly crowd to pray and donate their last penny?

Forceful, vigorous, energetic, eager, hearty: all words used to describe belief. However, a word which always applies is 'unarguable'. If each faith and doctrine is 'the true belief', then surely they cancel out each others' credibility. If any one of them is discredited, either by discoveries that contradict their scriptures, or beliefs that contradict reality, then why should any of the faiths be any less fanciful than the others?

But before we investigate the bases, ethics and validity-factors involved in these faiths, a little tactful diplomacy might be called for. So, now for something completely different.

Chapter 18

This is Where it Starts to Become Autobiographical

The unbiased viewpoint. Essentially unconnected, and how this came to be.

The subject-matter of this chapter is different, so a little explanation is required to illustrate its fundamental relevance to the text.

This chapter provides an insight into my own credibility and grounds for my views on certain subjects. My views are quite radically different from traditional understandings, so why should they carry any more plausibility than conformist opinions? For example, when studying a subject as sensitive as religion, what justification can I claim for my own observations? Are they any more sound and rational than those under scrutiny?

There is a naturally disdainful reaction when we are confronted by unconventional opinions which might refute any lifelong understandings. This book provides a logically-sound submission, simply explained and easily followed.

We as human beings, with all our idiosyncrasies, are self-defeatingly under the influence of an inbuilt refusal to accept anything other than that which we have been told in our formative years! We'll come back to analysing imprinting later. Assuming that the principle regarding the strength of our formative-age conditioning is not disputed, there is an essential requirement for objective weighing-up of obvious and unconscious prejudices and implications from this influence.

It is quite undeniable in the light of today's vastly more enlightened world that being taught something by someone who will have been similarly formatively informed does not mean that it still is an authentic piece of information and has to be believed without question! In fact it is only with today's level of knowledge that we are in a position to see through these outdated stories with informed and enlightened eyes. Teachers may have provided us and our ancestors with this "knowledge" with the very best of intentions, but that does not mean that knowledge is necessarily true. It is important that this provision is understood before we continue.

Beginning with Darwin's revelations, there are already many logical conclusions which directly contradict and disprove some of the stories printed in the Bible, previously understood to be factual. For example, there is the geologically confirmable evolution-sequence which contradicts the created in Seven Days story and the wealth of astronomical, scientific and geological discoveries which oppose and erode a substantially increasing amount of the Bible's "facts." How long will it take for the realities of life to put the fabricated and unsubstantiated fiction of the Bible into its proper perspective? With new facts all the time, how long does it have to take before the penny finally drops?

Of course, there is the matter of different religions, and how so many of them seem to contradict each other to different extents. Without wishing to appear disrespectful, I do observe that not only do many of them oppose, belittle or discredit each other without much provocation, but each faithful believer remains convinced they are right. So many religions hold beliefs which are partially or completely at odds, so how can it be anything other than fundamental logic that there's only one of them which can actually be valid. This makes all the others fallacious.

Bearing in mind the hallucinatory, "dream"-based foundations which form the bases of most religions, and also how flimsy and susceptible to political or other manipulations the theme and content of their understanding can be, it's not really surprising how varying and incompatible they all are! With the fact that many religions depend upon sacred texts which are increasingly shown to be mistaken or misapplied, then how can anyone be certain that any of the scriptures are factual? In short, if there is any evidence to substantiate any of these tales, then where is it? This entire issue is looked into in a lot more investigative depth later.

The above rationale is simply the application of logical and realistic reasoning, but I hope that it might open up or underline some niggling doubts that might even now be starting to germinate in the reader's mind.

To expand upon this point, it could also logically be argued that if any one of these easily-hypothesised faiths with its own equally-adamant believers were, in reality, to represent the sole exemplification of the "truth" then, surely, it would be persuasively-evident that that particular religion's followers were better-blessed than the average?

They would certainly be conspicuous, enjoying the rewards of their faith. But do they? Is it a mere coincidence that it seems to be within the confines of more fundamentalist or dogmatic faiths with their strict, segregationist disciplines and practices, that they are increasingly unable to conceal the prevalence of their paupers and beggars? Surely these poor souls are not just the unbelievers? "The Will of Allah", "God works in Mysterious ways" and "Karmic debt" seem to be just a few of the convenient clichés that are usually put forward. How do they explain away a one-belief Heaven, Paradise, Nirvana, Valhalla or other adopted name that they might like to bandy around, and the fate of all the animals that die? Are they (as non-believers) relegated to some sort of inferno?

What about the incredible coincidence of one's just happening to be born into a family that follows the "true" faith when, all around, there are others following other faiths with no less conviction and no more evidence...

To summarise which, if any, of the faiths is the "true" belief, there really isn't any evidence or positive testament that any one of the many religions has more validity than the others. As it appears to the impartial eye, if there is a faith which stands head and shoulders above the rest, then there certainly is no visible evidence of it. Surely, it would show somehow? Perhaps it's just that the worshippers of the real "truth" like to keep their good, favoured lives under wraps for some reason. Wherever they might be, they don't seem to be endorsing their faith with any obvious evidence of reward! Logically, then, if there were so many enjoying the spoils of their faith, they would not be able to deny it.

How much longer can observations like this be denied?

Chapter 19

Qualification and Competence

Why should my viewpoint be more credible than the traditional one?

The previous chapter might not have seemed to be fully compliant with the autobiographical depiction that headed it, but it could have been clouded by the text's careful approach to subjects that are paradoxically both 'taken-for-granted' but underlyingly 'open-to-question'. Whilst trying not to alienate the reader by implying that it is in any way denigrating to believe that which was taught in one's formative years, it needs to be recognised that the validity of these teachings is not above being challenged. Nor does it detract from the integrity of those who furnished this information. They provided, with the best of intentions, the knowledge of the time. We are now, for the first time, in possession of knowledge which allows us to re-designate the superseded knowledge into its proper context: a rich part of our social heritage, without which we would have no cultural standards.

However, in this modern age of supportable new information, especially where it contests outdated beliefs, we sometimes have to remind ourselves about the conditions that prevailed when the old beliefs were contrived. This is another issue which is looked into in some depth, with some judicial perception. Meanwhile, back to the now "autobiographical" situation.

Why am I in a position to enable me to see things in a way others don't? The origin is nothing more unusual than my atypical upbringing. As a result of this, my impartial and 'unorchestrated' outlook on life provided me with a fundamentally different point of view, as I shall explain.

I have a strong, probably inherited and perhaps old fashioned sense of responsibility, with the drive to stand against any conventional or traditional opinions and expectations if or when I feel it to be justifiable or warranted. This is a principle which applies whatever the unpopularity or unrest that might be provoked as a result of my taking any such stance. For me, applying principle is paramount. My background will probably explain and clarify the rationale behind this contention.

I was born in 1938, the son of a Jewish father, Sam, and Church of England mother, Stella. I was lucky that both of my parents had undogmatic views about religious principles. None of the usual pressures were applied to me at any time. This left me with the unique option of being able to decide for myself which, if any, religious pathways I would choose from if, or when, I ever felt the need to. Now, how many children can claim to have had that privilege and freedom?

My early schooling at Gants Hill, Ilford, provided me with all the usual Christian disciplines at the early-morning assemblies and religious education lessons. In order to balance that, my father introduced me to the local synagogue where, for a while, I attended their shul (the equivalent of the Christian Sunday-school) at which the basics of the Jewish faith were taught to me. However, with the benefit of my open-minded frame of reference, neither of the two religious options appeared less capricious than the other. In fact, with the contrasting priorities, the underlying disparities, the way in which the foundational stories of (all) faiths were invariably presented as being unquestionably factual despite being based on (as it seemed to me) flimsy foundations and their even flimsier vulnerability to falsification, then a sceptical outlook soon established itself as being the only one for me.

After that conclusion, I viewed all theological activities and proclamations through more questioning eyes. The unrealistic tales of the familiar religions were as implausible as other faiths. The belief-devaluing experiences of my observations of everyday life accumulated. The entire subject of religion was placed into a debatable perspective for me..

But although the school's history and science lessons often openly contradicted the same school's frequently-quoted holy scripts, nobody else appeared to notice or seemed prepared to question these anomalies. The impression that penetrated and lodged itself in my young mind was that those scriptural texts, although known to be at the least of very questionable authenticity, were for some reason allowed to be above being challenged on the most obvious implausibility. The faithful believers preferred to overlook or ignore their inconsistencies. By pretending otherwise, it was almost as if the discrepancies lost their credibility. Validating the soundness of any discipline that carried a religious connotation meant that any logic that would undermine the basic soundness of religious ethics in a normal argument, was rendered null and void. Implausible stories remained above contention and were referred to as fact. This, too, applies in politics.

However, as life unfolded and increasingly more religious incongruities came to light, my scepticism hardened. I could see a factor which appeared to be common to all the faiths that I looked into, and this was that they ultimately depended historically upon mere tutorials for both their conception and soundness. Also, that the 'choice' about which actual belief any person's entire life might revolve around would be in virtually all cases, dictated by where they happened to be born and which of the various faiths their parents happened to follow and believe in. This is all very circumstantial, but people remain immovably fixated. Tutorials, differing scriptures based on word of mouth at some time in their evolution, and the tales themselves, often admitted to being of a dream or hallucination-based source.

Word of mouth in itself is derisory. Everyone knows a story can change from one end of the street to the other! All tales in the oral tradition were often not permanently recorded for centuries! It all appeared to be beyond belief in my eyes, but others just accepted it all as if they'd seen it for themselves and there could be no doubt about it all! But there was, they just were told that there was! The records themselves, as the history lessons were happy to reveal, weren't reliable. They were known to have been tampered with for political reasons. How often were these infringements not even known about? When the other pupils and teachers cheerfully quoted scriptures as facts, it staggered me how gullible everybody else seemed to be. How could <u>any</u> doctrine based on such flimsy testimony even be given the time of day? All the "evidence" would be immediately dismissed by a court of law.

That is how I came to my convictions about the religions I had been introduced to. It seemed to me that because everyone else believed it, nobody wanted to think outside it. The same concept applied to all faiths. They gained their strength from awe, fear, stability and parental guidance– at least, that's how I saw it!

This outlook on life was not confined to my religious views. In fact, I did not have an aversion to religious beliefs in themselves, but the way their believers literally followed all they'd been told to believe, eliminating any reason to think outside the box! This opened my mind to the thesis that all the 'faithful' are effectively shutting their minds to anything else that <u>might</u> be out there!

So, that was my belief – not anti-religion (although I didn't understand the obdurate blindness that seemed to transfix some) but open-mindedness on the subject. If any thesis had evidence to validate it, I should have accepted it. I had seen and was aware about the mysteries of life and all of its unknowns. Religion provides an easy answer for those who don't want to make the effort to look further. How easy it is to take on board that which one is told as a fact in childhood, that which provides a convenient and comfortable solution to all life's unanswerables. However, such an easy way out wasn't for me. Cogency and common sense was the protocol which patterned the future ahead of me. It paid off.

That is how this outlook first impacted my world, and a non-aligned, objective way of understanding and confrontational life gradually evolved. That may answer the matter of qualification and competence.

This chapter is somewhat introverted, but its purpose has been to explain how the early teaching and formative years of my life gave me an unusually objective way of looking at things. The psychology and credibility of this viewpoint should become clear soon.

Chapter 20

Time for a Little Rationalisation and Validation

How can matters of such importance be based on such flimsy foundations?

There is one, major difficulty in writing a book like this, which is putting down on paper something the reader needs to know about but might rather not read! It contains some very unwelcome facts about life. The 'major difficulty' is keeping the text readable and interesting without frightening off the reader: a careful balance of 'unputdownability' against some unpleasant observations and deductions!

However, there's one aspect that makes my job a little less uphill. That is the conscience element: where the reader has uncovered sufficient detail about the threat to overcome the unsettling nature of the contents in order to see it all through to the bitter end! From my point of view, it would have been easier to do nothing and hope that someone else would pick up the drum and bang it. But the easy way out isn't for me. I have a strong social conscience and I hope that a similar sense will spur the reader onwards.

This brings me to a discussion of relevance.

The subject matter and the conclusions drawn in the previous chapters might appear to be utterly irrelevant to some. However, the point has to be made. If one regards the beliefs and understandings imparted in one's childhood as being infallible, then all of those anecdotes cannot be wrong. Why should this be? Nobody can be accused of wrong-doing if it related to them by a parent at the age when everything that such a mentor imparts seems unquestionable.

The same authenticity factor applies to the mentor, whose own mentor, and their mentor and their mentors before them all perceive the anecdotes as genuine.

The same level of unquestioned acceptance applies to the anecdotes themselves. This includes all religious beliefs. First, I ask that the possibility of those anecdotes should not be dismissed as infallible. In other words, I ask the reader to keep an open mind for a few more chapters.

Returning to the previous chapter, the purpose of illustrating my rationale for seeing life as I do is to show the <u>difference</u> between that which is actually in place and that which registers as being there after having been primed from childhood. This might sound a little unlikely, but it must be conceded that the resulting perceptions don't necessarily match up! For example, children expect to see just one Santa Claus, some adults are told and still believe that it can be "too cold to snow", or that the world is only a few thousand years old, and for ages everyone <u>thought</u> that the sun and stars revolved around the Earth. But we can be wrong, or misinformed, and must bear that in mind.

Nevertheless, some may conclude, despite the strength and logic of my submissions, that these observations should be cast aside. Why? What could be reason to maintain such a shuttered viewpoint? Could it be that these observations specifically contradict the formatively-ingrained beliefs which so many are firmly <u>told</u> must never be disputed whatever the appeal of any alternative enticements?

I return to my open outlook and how my life evolved to facilitate an ultimate use of it for advantageous purposes.

I begin with my 'religious education' lessons at school. My uninfluenced mind meant that the universally-accepted tutorials didn't quite 'sit easy' with me. I couldn't understand how hugely significant and life-influencing conclusions could be taken so irrevocably such flimsy bases. It was clear that in pre-printing days, all of these motivationally-crucial stories had no other way of being circulated than word of mouth. Word of mouth just isn't a safe and accurate way of keeping the facts precise. My history lessons directly contradicted my R.E lessons, explaining how documented evidence took centuries to be put into print. This served well in my eyes to paradoxically illustrate both the strength and the weakness of such belief.

Nor could I quite understand how all holy scriptures should be so blindly accepted by their followers as undeniable actualities when, if that same believer had been born into the house next door, then a completely different religion might have been theirs for life!

It was all so vague and questionable, but it was emulated so rigidly, even though there was absolutely no positive evidence whatsoever to support these beliefs and understandings! In other words, they are not a sufficiently reliable and fundamentally sound basis on which to establish a lifelong dedication. A "chance landing" can absolutely determine the entire purpose of a person's life and its devotion to a particular faith. In some cases, people are actually prepared to give their lives for religious causes! This might sound prejudiced to some, but surely prejudice is the direct result of any persuasion rather than the complete absence of any such directive.

So, that's how I rationalised and developed my open-mindedness about religion. Indeed, open-mindedness is the perfect description for the situation I adopted. The maxim by which I firmly stood was that evidence is the essential requisite for certainty. It appeared to be common sense to abide by the principle that, until such time as proper and corroborated evidence could be provided, then there was no known faith which carried the credibility my sense of realism demanded. A non-aligned, unprejudiced and open receptivity gradually formed the framework of my perspective on life in general, as my formative years passed through adolescence to adulthood.

My pragmatic viewpoint on religions in general at that time meant the basic credibility and importance of the Church as a discipline slowly became inconsequential. Others might have felt the need to support it but, whilst respecting others' convictions or inducements, for me there was absolutely no need of it in my life or outlook. At least, not yet! It just played no part other than the place I would occasionally be expected to go for other peoples' ceremonial and social occasions, and where my observations served to endorse my line of thinking.

To summarise, a conscious decision had been made and was being followed: that of actively keeping a completely open mind on the subject of religion. I did not dismiss it as merely fallacious or unverifiable, but equally did not blindly follow any faiths until such time as something which could be firmly substantiated by clear evidence came into my life. This is the view that seemed to me to be the only sensible and mature approach to be adopted, mindful of all the previously-mentioned disparities. This almost indifferent outlook strengthened with the passage of time and with all of the experiences of life as they evolved.

Meanwhile, the conception about others' beliefs had engraved itself into my mind. It seemed to be that religion is almost robotically entrenched with life-directing beliefs and rituals, determined by nothing more than the country, area, even the door behind which a person happens to be born. In my mind it just didn't add up to an intelligent solution. To further the point, if a person's life is patterned by a decision of this sort, then should they not make the decision themselves when they have enough knowledge and experience of life to make a valid choice?

The important issue to be understood is how the way of thinking emerging in my mind evolved from my not being parentally influenced into any faith. From that seed, the rationale which grew and flourished was to become essential in my life.

Chapter 21

Back Down to Earth

A little personal history

As the previous chapter tried to emphasise, my psychological patterning, (or, to be more accurate, the line of thinking which resulted from my NOT being parentally patterned or influenced) is a significant fundamental of this book's message. The same applies, of course, to the thinking behind my doubts in the religious disciplines which have such an immense influence of the lives of others. This emphasis underscores the need for the reader to properly understand the logic which covers the subjects about to be uncovered, and the reason for this will be clear soon.

Except for my little-known ideas and unusual viewpoint, my life followed a fairly conventional and unexciting pattern. I progressed from serving five years as an apprentice draughtsman at the Bankside House headquarters of the C.E.G.B., to meaningful employment at the Ford Motor Company's Research and Engineering Centre at Dunton in Essex.

It was whilst working there in the 1960s and 70s as a design engineer that my long-standing enthusiasm for (at first spectating and then competing in) the sport of motor-cycle racing became a big part of my life. How is that relevant to matters of real importance like overpopulation? All will become clear. Although it might require a little understanding and patience, this section is really essential as it serves to illustrate an issue crucial to the entire context of this book.

For those who might not be familiar with the motorcycle racing scenario, it involves several different classes of machinery. One of these is the "sidecar" category. Briefly, these machines are derived from the conventional, road-going solo bike we are all familiar with, except that the sidecar touring bodywork is replaced on racers by little more than a flat platform between the 'bike' itself and the third wheel. The supporting crew-member is carried on this panel, quite literally leaping about to position himself in the best place in order to keep the high-speed vehicle as stable as he can! It might sound crazy, but the "passengers" virtually made the sidecar or "three-wheeler" class of motorcycle racing probably the most spectacular form of high-speed action on the motor-racing circuits!

I became involved as a driver while I was on the Design staff at Fords. At first I competed using conventional outfits, but then my unorthodox way of thinking presented a new design initiative to me. "Why not", I thought, "change from using a conventional motorcycle engine in the racer, and redesign the entire machine to incorporate a Ford-based car engine instead?"

What were the advantages of this? For a start, the access to design-details and parts for the Ford engine would be a huge asset, but the 1,000cc and 1,200cc engines which normally powered the "Anglias" and "Cortinas" of the time were particularly sturdy engines. As many race-engine builders and developers of the time knew, these made a very reliable and 'easily-tuneable' base for some extremely powerful car-racing engines.

If my Ford-based motorcycle idea proved to be a viable one, then any of these power-packs would easily "slot-in". The project's power-potential, as far as the world of motorcycle-racing was concerned, was unparalleled.

First, I had to design a machine that could both carry the heavy car-engine so that it didn't get in the way of the driver or passenger, and would be in such a position that its heavy weight wouldn't prejudice stability. That's where logic crept in. Why not position the long engine lengthwise along the centreline of the machine, with the passenger in his normal position (laying face-down along the straights) on one side of the engine, with the driver on the other side (and completely new for motorcycles of any sort) also laying in a face-down attitude, arms-forward to the handlebars, feet-backward to the brake and gear change controls! Without having the orthodox racers' inbuilt disadvantage of the driver's having to crouch down and make himself as small as possible _above_ his engine, the new engine-position meant that there was nothing underneath the driver, so down he could go! It was an idea that had not ever been tried before but, apart from the enormous power-advantage potential, it was also immediately evident that there were substantial benefits to be gained from the weight-distribution and streamlining aspects.

To put all of this concept into actuality was clearly no small undertaking, but it was a challenge! It would entail the designing and building of a particularly unique project. Such a concept has not been matched either before or since the fifteen years or so during which it was raced. As I saw it, the project had the very exciting potential to make quite a big impression in the motorcycle racing world.

This is a very abbreviated outline of how my unusual way of viewing a particular situation initiated the start of a life-changing project. In fact the above is nothing more than the shortest-possible outline of how my individual viewpoint on life in general provided me with a huge opening in my life.

There is a contextual value to this section. It describes some of the examples of my unfettered way of viewing situations (my parents' achievement), but the value of these will no doubt be gauged as the book unfolds.

It was a perfectly natural thing for me to consider the use of Ford car engines in racers while working in Ford's engine design and test area. There, I could make use of all the other innovations and advantages I have mentioned. I have only briefly described the hugely significant advantage that the use of specifically Ford car engines provided to the scheme. Whilst availability of all the design details of the 'standard' or un-tuned engines was of immense value, the biggest asset by far was that of the smaller Ford engines being used in the mid-60s by the majority of race-engine companies. The reason for their popularity was that the basic "Kent" engine (the company's codename for the 'straight-four' used in their Anglias and

Cortinas at that time) was a fundamentally sturdy little unit with the capacity to safely produce and carry far more power than it never needed to in its domestic guise. Of course, for that very reason, engine-tuners found it ideal as a basis upon which to build their seriously-competitive power units. This meant that if, as hoped, my prototype machine designed and built around a bog-standard Ford Anglia engine proved my concept to be a viable one, then the opportunities for incorporating engines with power-output figures unheard-of in motorcycling were immense.

Inevitably all of these ambitious plans presented more than just a few problems. The most obvious one was that of the sheer mass and weight of the car engine as compared to that of bike engines. This was put to best use by the idea of mounting the 'lump' right on the epicentre of the three road-contact points. By positioning it lengthways along the centreline of the machine between the driver and the passenger, then the engine's physical intrusion was minimal.

The next complication was, however, a lot more technical. The transmission-line or "power-train", i.e. the route or the power-line along which the output from the engine has to run in order to make to driving-wheel rotate and, by this means, definitively and safely drive the machine forward.

With any 'normal' racing outfit, a standard or conventional bike gearbox with its "positive-stop" simple up/down foot-pedal gear-change system would have been quite capable of transmitting the standard Anglia's power, would have been very easy to incorporate and would have presented no obvious selection-problems. The headache, however, was that there was no motorcycle gearbox anywhere that would be anything like sturdy enough to transmit the power and the torque that would be produced by the engines that were expected to be used later in the project's progress.

So, a gearbox with a big capacity but light weight was called for and, although it sounds like a big prerequisite, the Ford-engines' use in many car-racing formulae provided an easy answer. A company which traded under the name of the Hewland Gearbox Company had already designed a unit for the rear-engined 'Formula 2' racing class which, in utilising the magnesium 'shell' from the Volkswagen 'Beetle' car gearbox, provided not only the light unit as needed but, in being designed for use in just such a rear-engined vehicle, the VW box also incorporated a differential unit which turned the rotation of the engine-power through 90-degrees. For F2 use it was ideal, but, very conveniently for my design, it provided precisely the rotation-direction required for the project's rear wheel. So, from there, back to bike principles with a heavy-duty rear driving-chain, and a very big design-problem had virtually resolved itself!

For the technically-minded, the standard VW gearbox was designed as a three-shaft, all-indirect unit with four forward gears being carried on two of the layshafts, and the car's reverse-gear on the other one. Selection was made by one selector-arm that was first turned to engage with a slot near the end of one of the three shafts and then, by 'pushing-in' or 'pulling-out', it engages any one of the gears as required. Hewland's modification, without the need for a reverse gear for their specific customers, used all three shafts for forward gears, and so were able to sell their boxes with a choice of almost any gear-ratio for a six-speed gear unit! They also manufactured a ready-made "adaptor-plate" to fit the gearbox straight onto the Ford engine and so the set-up all fell into place.

However, that was only the start of the ambitious project; the next problem was how to change gear <u>by foot</u>, bike-fashion!

With a 'car' gearbox designed for changing gear via the "gearlever-left-in-place-in-a-double-H" system (i.e. as in a normal car), this meant that for the essential 'bike-type foot-change operation, some serious modifications were called for!

The only practical answer was to some way convert Hewland's system into a bike-style "positive-stop" method (which, at that time, didn't exist in car-racing). Here is how it was achieved.

Inside the selector-chamber (which would normally have carried the "selector arm" as above), a steel cylinder or drum was installed so that it could rotate on its bearings around the three previously-mentioned gearshafts. With the drum turning on the same axis-alignment as the three gearshafts and with it's being activated through plus-or-minus 60-degrees by each stroke of a tangential operating-shaft that engaged (via spring-loaded teeth) with one of six castellations that had been machined into the top edge of the drum, then the three gearshafts had only to engage with a cam-track on the inside or the drum to achieve the necessary sequential gear changes. In other words, as the drum turned through one-sixth of a revolution either clockwise or anticlockwise as required (an easy foot-operated task), then if each gearshaft <u>in its turn</u> could be moved by the cam-track so that each stroke of the operating-shaft either pushed-in or pulled-out just one of the gearshafts, then that's how it would work.

This was achieved by the method of brazing a small spindle across the top of each gearshaft. These spindles carried small needle-roller bearings that engaged with the cam-track formed on the inside face of the drum, and the three spindles each with their own engagement needle-rollers set at 120-degrees to move in or out in turn as the rotating camtrack moved around them one way or the other! So, how was the camtrack formed? By the drum's having made for it a second, tight-fitting internal sleeve, that was first drilled to accept rivets to hold it locked positively in place in-side the outer drum then, *before* the rivets were fitted, the camtrack was cut into the inner sleeve of the drum so that when it was riveted securely into back into place, the newly-separated top and bottom halves of the inner sleeve retained their relative positions and hence formed the upper and lower runs of the new camtrack. This may or may not sound simple, though getting it all to work created lots of development problems. Eventually the selection of one of six gears through a simple up-or-down foot-pedal movement was achieved. Although this system was pioneered quite a few decades ago, it might be of interest to those familiar with today's racing (particularly in view and relevance of the "unorthodox open-mindedness" context of this particular section of the book) that this is precisely the form of gear changing that has recently been so revolutionary in car-racing today.

What they now call the "paddle" system allows any number of gear-ratios to be used without having to remember what gear you're in, so you can change gear immediately and accurately. Bikes, of course, have had this facility for ages, and because of this, racing bikes have been free to use closer-ratio gearboxes with more power being able to be squeezed from a given engine-size by the use of "peakier" power-curves, inlet and exhaust gas-resonating at specific bands and cam-profiles changed to exploit this valuable capability.

Also, gear changes can be "played by ear", by the rev-limiter or the tachometer. All of this has only recently been innovated in the car competition world.

Another interesting problem that the prototype of this project brought to light was the steering/front-suspension configuration. The obstacle which had to be resolved was how to innovate a system which did its task whilst keeping all its components below the (laying flat) driver's sightline. Now, the smallest-diameter front wheel available which could accommodate the essential racing-standard tyres, was that which used the 10-inch diameter racing-mini rims. With these wheels and tyres fitted on the racer, it meant that an outside-diameter of about 19-inches had to be catered for. With the minimum-possible suspension movement of about plus 2-inches, then the eye-level had to be set at a minimum of 21 inches to clear the top face of the tyre 'under suspension'. The result was that there was absolutely no room left for the luxury of suspension-forks! However, for the purpose of establishing whether or not the project was worth pursuing, the prototype was fitted with a conventional bike-type telefork system, albeit designed to have the shortest-possible length. This "lashup" severely affected both the driving visibility and the streamlining object of the project, but at least it was on the road!

Once the project had been given a season's very enlightening assessment, and was obviously of great interest to the media, the result was a completely new model's being designed and built in my Chelmsford garage. This time the problem of the teleforks' visibility handicap was resolved by eliminating them. How? By mounting the front wheel (using the two ends of the central spindle) and with each end of the spindle's being mounted on a section of a low, near horizontal supporting disc so that when the front wheel was turned to steer the outfit, it slid between the top and bottom faces of a P.T.F.E. low-friction "sandwich". It proved to be just a bit too "sticky" for the light steering necessary, but it proved that the idea of a disc-mounted wheel worked.

So, using the same "steered-disc" idea, a system was designed that replaced the P.T.F.E. pads with four "clusters" of needle-roller bearings that carried the supporting disc's chamfered edge between the 45-degree-angled clusters in adjustable clamps inside the suspension-loop.

This was much better, but too flimsy. It failed in a meeting at the Chivenor circuit. Nevertheless, before it failed, a season's competition demonstrated that the novel "steered disc" system was a very viable one. Radically simplified for this text, the problem of supporting the steered-disc had finally been resolved by the use of a suitably-mounted 18-inches diameter ballbearing assembly to replace the four weak "clusters". This is how the project achieved its steering system without visibility over the front wheel being inhibited by any suspension or steering linkage or ancillaries, and the photographs will help to make a difficult description more undertsandable. That was one challenge which had been resolved thanks to open mindedness. There was another which needs explaining: chain drive.

The Hewland transaxle's inbuilt differential was simply braze-locked to, in effect, form a 90-degree bevel-drive out through just one side of the normally-two take-off sides, this driving (via a rubber "doughnut"-type universal joint) through a second in-line shaft that rotated on bearings mounted inside a fixed, tubular chassis-member. This second shaft had the chain-sprocket on one end and a brake-disc on the other, and a 3/4" x 3/4" duplex, heavy-duty chain did the rest.

With the 'bike-type "swinging-arm" rear suspension carried by two Ford conn-rod bigends that had been designed and built-in to the system's assembly so that they pivoted or oscillated in special channel-sections machined into the same "fixed tubular chassis-member", then the hard-working drive-chain between the drive-shaft and the rear-wheel sprockets, as a consequence of its input-sprocket's being mounted on the same axis as that of the suspension, was totally unaffected by any of the race-machine's suspension-movement and so remained in constant tension.

Something else which might help to illustrate the purpose of this chapter is those "new" adjustable aerofoils that are making quite an important impact on the Formula 1 scene now. Our Mark 5 machine introduced such a speed-sensitive, hydraulically-operated, brake-actuated airflow "spoiler" onto the circuits; and this, would you believe, was first raced on the 27th of June, in 1977!

Powered by Ford engines, and with its unarguably-unique layout and design, what else could we possibly have called it other than the "Unorfordox"?

This section is intended to illustrate nothing more than how the open-mindedness of my upbringing imparted on my life, More to the point, it shows the result of the cognisance and uninhibited-thinking I developed from <u>not</u> being fed preconditioned beliefs and understandings. This unusual insight provided me with the foresight to see problems or situations from a more-remote, less-conventional viewpoint. As a result, I answered them with the application of a little more logic than the 'programmed' eyes might have been able to bring to the situation.

Chapter 22

So What was all that Waffle About Racing For?

A full and explicit answer to this question

So, the technicalities might be finished with but, for the sake of the curiosity of one or two of the more cogitative biking 'elders' who might have been interested in bike-racing around that time, or who might remember it being mentioned in the papers or on TV between the late 1960s through to the early 1980s, they might like to know what was the eventual outcome of all that effort? Well, that's another, somewhat long story, already written and is hoped to be published shortly. The entire reason for the project being put under the spotlight is to illustrate an imperative but very elementary principle, and that which has been described in the last few chapters should have adequately demonstrated the issue in question. In Particular, it demonstrates how a non-indoctrinated mind can be left free to make decisions which haven't been subliminally-guided by formative-years 'knowledge'. In fact, the purpose of the technical-section is to show, in a way which can be understood by the non-technical, issues a little 'specialist' in nature that a 'free mind' can see, and a 'doctored mind' cannot. That might sound a little discriminatory, so I'll put it another way. The idea is to show how, (with the evidence of the project's success,) certain aspects of absolutely anyone's observations, thinking and decision-making, will be free to see the facts of life in general from an entirely different perspective. They'll see things as they actually are rather than the way their parents have 'conditioned' them to see and, if parents themselves, what they'd expect their own kids to see! Does that sound a bit unlikely? Well, please read on. Should you still be in doubt, there are several clear instances soon to be put forward which might put things into a vitally different perspective.

In my case, the life-changing gift my parents provided me with left my mind open to see past conventional-thinking. And, as a direct result of this, I have been able to recognise and exploit some unique and ground-breaking ideas. A great deal of care has been taken in the previous chapters to show this as clearly as possible and to demonstrate how this came to be put into effect with the pioneering ideas, i.e. the 'Unorfordox' project. This might sound boastful, but the intention is to positively show, with evidence, how the mind of an ordinary man without special education or abilities can observe that which is about him in a completely different perspective to virtually all the other people that were and are around him. How? Simply as a result of not being impressed as a child to 'see' what I was told and was expected to 'see' and, more fundamentally, to believe what I had been told was "the truth" and not to be questioned! Sensible?

The problem is that, on paper, all of this disclosure of one's own exploits can appear little more than vanity, but there really is no other way to illustrate the outcome of my open-mindedness. The project and all of the innovations which went into making it are the actual material evidence which validates the thesis of how open-mindedness can work. Many people just don't realise that formative conditioning can virtually dictate what they think. It's only when this is realised that sometimes life-pivotal free-minded decisions, such as my project, can be acknowledged and exploited.

For the benefit of those who might still have doubts about the strength and the hidden intransigence of formative years conditioning, the very unawareness of its existence is the biggest reason for its being implemented so often and so blindly.

Take, for example, something simple and inoffensive like the phobias that become imprinted in a child when they see an adult scream in fear at the sight of a harmless spider, or leap on a chair because there's an innocuous mouse somewhere in the room! Are these the intelligent actions of an epitome of common sense? Hardly, but it's what embeds subliminally in the child's mind. The child grows up with a completely irrational phobia deeply embedded in its mind. Ready to be passed on in the same way to the next generation. If that isn't 100% proof of formative years subliminal intransigence, then what is?

This is all proof of the existence of something we have to recognise before we can put it into perspective, and then rein it in.

After all, this is just the way in which all of those parental beliefs (aware of them or not) are imprinted and so on <u>before</u> a child is old and aware enough to work out the logic or the rights and wrongs of the subject. This passes unnoticed, whilst unquestioned beliefs gradually become rigidly-fixed by permeation through the years, almost by default. "Conditioned", "patterned", "indoctrinated" – call it what you will, but beliefs and expectations are inflicted on nearly all children in this way, through their formative years and beyond. Once they're in, it takes a lot of convincing to move them out! For example, do you remember being told what was the "right" thing to believe in, and what nasty things happen to those who don't? What about all those early-morning assemblies every day at school, where you were expected to chant prayers parrot-fashion, to sing sometimes incomprehensible hymns, listen to implausible readings and say "amen" after everything, all firmly cementing the principle in formative minds? How can this <u>not</u> be conditioning? Isn't all that routine a fact of young life?

If you "do the right thing" and go to church as you'd be "trained" to do, whatever religion, is not this exactly the same imprinting, just reinforced?

The important fact, though, is that I was different. This was not <u>my</u> accomplishment, but my parents'. It was the direct outcome of being allowed an un-blinkered upbringing by my parents that I was left the freedom to make up my own mind when I was ready (and informed enough!) to do so. My parents just provided me with the encouragement to listen to, and take in the wealth of different stories, experiences and information, to weigh up for myself the dependability or, where relevant, the importance of these and, in my *own time*, decide for myself just what was the most sensible line to follow.

It was almost as a natural outcome of this latitude that my beliefs about religion were left in limbo.

That freedom allowed me to develop what I regarded as a logical and natural outlook on all the aspects of life with an unbiased theological point of view, one that is normally parentally-denied and religiously-marshalled to children, even today! This is precisely the principle that I was able to put to such good use through my life whilst employed in design engineering at Ford's, into and out of my motorcycling years, and during many more interesting episodes in my life. All told, many valuable outcomes were reaped from the sowing of just one elementary seed of freedom.

That is the purpose of this chapter: to demonstrate to the reader the almost dictatorial way that the majority of receptive young minds are deprived of their freedom of thought and self-decision. This mind-manipulation (for that's what it is) usually influences or determines the course of an individual's entire life. However, when unrestrained by such early indoctrination, one's thinking is left free to develop along its own level of investigation and reasoning. That is precisely the criterion that establishes the credibility of this entire book and the horrific conclusion it forecasts.

The Mark 1 in 1967 prototype – a very basic fabrication to
test the idea's feasibility
(Passenger: Mick Wooler)

Mark 1 at Brands Hatch
(Passenger: Dane Rowe)

Mark 2

Mark 3

Mark 4

Mark 5

Mark 6

This photograph shows machine and transporter mounted (with wheel-locking van ramp) on "start-rollers", which can fire-up and run the machine (no starter-motor) without having to bump-start it.

All paddock shots of the Mark 6 Unorfordox

The final, Mark 6, Unorfordox. I am demonstrating the central engine, the low, 'flat' driving position that it accommodates, and the obvious weight-distribution and streamlining benefits.

Details showing development of the 'peripheral' or 'circumferential' steering system (uniquely crucial in this project as sight-obstruction had to be taken into account).

Right. Scheme 1: The front wheel is mounted between two 'floating' sections of a common disc, each side's being sandwiched between PTFE (low-friction) laminates. It worked, but proved too 'sticky' as sensitive steering is vital.

Centre. Scheme 2: Replaced with the wheel mounted in a one-piece disc which turned between four clusters of needle-roller bearings angled to seat (two above and one below) on the disc's bevelled edge. Again, it worked well, but found to be too weak under heavy braking.

Bottom. The successful conclusion. Same principle but using one, large bearing instead of four 'clusters'. Details are shown on next page

Steering-system details.

Right: The drawing and working components of the 'cluster' concept. The wheel-carrying ring turns between the four sets of needle-roller bearings.

Left: This shows the "wheel-ring" in it's bearings, which can be seen mounted inside the front suspension-loop.

Right: Using the same principle, but with the four 'clusters' replaced by one, large circumferential bearing.

Left: Again, the assembled system, this time with the front wheel, showing how each spindle-end clamps in housings carried by the 'live' inner bearing-ring.

(About 1 mile from the Bellvue
WILDLIFE CENTRE you visited a
year or two ago!)
9th July 1991

Pontgoy,
Tyncelyn,
Blaenpennal, Aberystwyth,
Dyfed SY23 4TN

Tel: Bronant 626

David Bellamy Esq.,
C/o Public Relations Dept.,
BBC Television Centre,
LONDON W12 7RJ

Dear Mr. Bellamy (or David, if I may),

Ref. encl. "The TRUE Facts of Life".

I have just noticed in next week's Radio Times that you are
highlighting a subject that is very close to my own heart
and which, in my simple eyes, is dangerously under-rated.

I have put my feelings down in verse in an attempt to raise
awareness by creating interest before causing offence to
those (lets say) persons of more staid convictions and, as
it appears that my fears are shared by yourself, perhaps I
might presume in asking if you would spare the time to read
through my offering?

Ulterior motive? Well, I am desperately looking for an
outlet in order to broadcast as loudly and as widely as possible what I consider to be a blindly-concealed growing danger.
Perhaps, if you agree with my opinions and you consider the
quality of my effort to be worthy of your valuable attention,
maybe you could assist in some way, possibly by suggesting
how I can best achieve this?

Hoping to hear from you, and trusting that you might find
the enclosed to be of interest, I am

Yours sincerely,

Jack Hay.

Dear Jack

Super poem, ?

have taken a copy

Hope you keep the wolf
from

[signature]

Letter correspondence copy of original (1991) composition of the poem, as sent to David Bellamy, with his response.

TELEGRAM

Charge to pay — POST OFFICE — 49 — N° 365 — OFFICE STAMP
RECEIVED 15-01-743 8000 4538 + TSO TGMS LN
CHELMSFORD 12 JAN 70

FE116 4.55 LONDON TELEX PRIORITY 32 =

PRIORITY MR J LEVY 15 STJOHNS RD CHELMSFORD =

PLEASE RING BBC BLUE PETER OFFICE REVERSING
CHARGES 01-743 8000 EXT 4538 SOONEST STOP RE
YOUR THREE WHEEL VEHICLE = EDWARD BARNES
PRODUCER BLUE PETER +

Aberaeron Non-Denominational Spiritualist Church

'Non-denominational' means that, as a church, we acknowledge and welcome with equal warmth followers of every Faith. We worship only God; the choice of any person's ROUTE to God has to be a personal matter, and it is certainly not for us to make any conditions, or to impose any prejudices, in an attempt to influence anybody.

Welcome to our free-thinking and enlightened church

Registered Charity No. 1060640

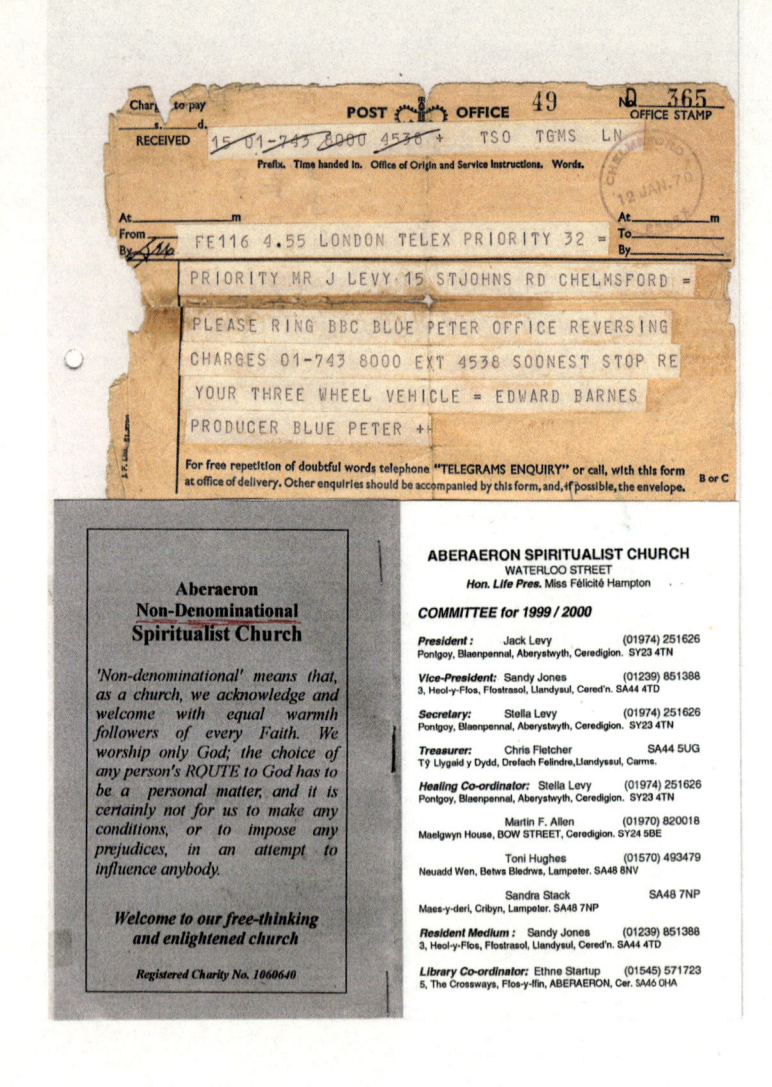

ABERAERON SPIRITUALIST CHURCH
WATERLOO STREET
Hon. Life Pres. Miss Félicité Hampton

COMMITTEE for 1999 / 2000

President: Jack Levy (01974) 251626
Pontgoy, Blaenpennal, Aberystwyth, Ceredigion. SY23 4TN

Vice-President: Sandy Jones (01239) 851388
3, Heol-y-Flos, Ffostrasol, Llandysul, Cered'n. SA44 4TD

Secretary: Stella Levy (01974) 251626
Pontgoy, Blaenpennal, Aberystwyth, Ceredigion. SY23 4TN

Treasurer: Chris Fletcher SA44 5UG
Tŷ Llygaid y Dydd, Drefach Felindre,Llandysul, Carms.

Healing Co-ordinator: Stella Levy (01974) 251626
Pontgoy, Blaenpennal, Aberystwyth, Ceredigion. SY23 4TN

Martin F. Allen (01970) 820018
Maelgwyn House, BOW STREET, Ceredigion. SY24 5BE

Toni Hughes (01570) 493479
Neuadd Wen, Betws Bledrws, Lampeter. SA48 8NV

Sandra Stack SA48 7NP
Maes-y-deri, Cribyn, Lampeter. SA48 7NP

Resident Medium: Sandy Jones (01239) 851388
3, Heol-y-Flos, Ffostrasol, Llandysul, Cered'n. SA44 4TD

Library Co-ordinator: Ethne Startup (01545) 571723
5, The Crossways, Ffos-y-ffin, ABERAERON, Cer. SA46 0HA

Just a little bit of personal history

Chapter 23

Freedom's Gift of Perception and Discernment

How this applies to religion

At this point the text becomes more incisive and possibly unsettling. As has been explained, one essential feature about this book is its progressive way of approaching certain issues. We are approaching a point where the message is of more importance than any distaste it might cause and, in any case, I hope that the earlier chapters will have prepared the newly-aware reader. It doesn't have to be pleasant news to be factual.

During my early childhood and school years, I became increasingly aware of all the conflicting "facts" that were proclaimed about different religions. The sheer incredibility factor of most narrated tales, the majority of which were unsupported by any basic evidential facts, and my increasing perception of just how numerous the various sects were, and how they were fuelled, helped inflame the healthy cynicism which would have such a big influence on my life. The strength of my findings were brought into focus: how a majority of the people I spoke to seemed to have been 'groomed' through their formative years. As such, they grew up to view the world and its many religions through their parents' eyes and the active prejudice of this was completely unseen.

So, as I saw it, this was the indoctrinated condition that prevailed all around me. It was almost as though most people were living in a defended, consecrated cage. Perfectly lucid people were living under the influence of little more than fairytales, but, they'd all been told that it was sinful to question such things, so they didn't!

That, at least, is how I saw the situation from my unusual, religiously uninfluenced vantage-point, and how it began to have an impact on my entire life.

Readers who might be disturbed by these personal observations and conclusions could easily dismiss them by saying my views are prejudiced. The definition of "open-mindedness, however, is "freedom from prejudice, readiness to consider new ideas". In other words, there is prejudice, but I am not the one who's practising it!

Let's take a break from the sensitive issue of religion and return to a more prosaic but nonetheless consequential passage through my life. Modesty forbids more elaboration than is absolutely necessary to illustrate essential points, however, to clearly demonstrate the most meaningful part of this book, and my lack of any remorse about the circumspection of my upbringing, then the mention of directly consequential accomplishments can be excused.

This very neatly reintroduces us to the unique, rewarding and interesting period in my blossoming career at Ford's, in conjunction with my closely-linked and publicly recognised racing project. It evolved and became more widely-known through its increasingly sophisticated and competitive design improvements (as shown by the photographs of its development on pages 130-135. The combination of a dedicated volunteer racing-team with supporters, the stream of sometimes unique design-challenges that presented themselves with the project's advancing progress, the many days spent testing them at various race-tracks and, ultimately, most in-season weekends in action with the team, then it can probably quite easily be visualised and acknowledged by even the least-interested reader how that level of adrenaline-charged lifestyle couldn't fail to have generated an exciting and unforgettable part of my life.

You're probably wondering how all of this is relevant to the story. The pertinence lies in this question: whether or not this was a result of the free-thinking that my parents allowed me, whether this enabled me to see problems more constructively?

Let's begin with the Unorfordox's conception. For a start, anything like the project's dramatic machine-layout had certainly never been built previously. It could have been done, but it wasn't, so by definition it was an innovation. It was not a copy of anything already or previously extant. All the mechanical ideas and innovations detailed in the last chapter are offered as indisputable evidence that clearing the mind of any preconceived ideas can lead to the simple and sensible application of clear, logical distraction-free thinking. I alone was able to see the construction of the Unorfordox as a simple and perfectly-logical design-step, and this was no mere coincidence. It is evidence of 'rational thinking as a result of having a clear mind', which is a classic case of cause and effect in operation.

The paradox is that one needs a clear mind in order to <u>see</u> the clutter. In order to actually re-orientate a predetermined mind, a lot of very convincing and persuasive evidence is necessary.

Returning to the background of the arguments about to be put forward: whilst the previous illustrations might provide the evidence of how de-conditioning the mind from its preconceived notions allows the creation of positive results, the same principle applies no less to other perspectives of life. This brings into contention the way that different sections of society are directed to perceive their answers to imponderable religious questions. "Imponderable" implies that these questions are not able to weighed or evaluated, which describes many of the assumptions we casually accept. Does that not sound absurd in today's world, in which more and more of the old precepts are being put into a realistic perspective rather than tales which might have been dreamed up to provide much-needed answers? Those answers both solved all the questions and were really irrefutable, when knowledge was sparse and when open minds were happy to hear something that couldn't be challenged. In addition to that, there's the matter of human exaggeration, so, realistically, is it not foolish to assume such knowledge such knowledge was not elaborated historically?

Chapter 24

Some Logical Conclusions

Delving just a little deeper into the logic and psychology

Blinkered eyes only see that which they are allowed to see. In this instance, that means people see that which they've been told they're expected to see. It's very similar to the paranoia disorder, where the patient is the very last person to concede that he is suffering from any delusions! Likewise, many of the minds that have been preconditioned aren't even aware that such a situation exists, or find it a lot more comfortable to deny it. However, before any blinkers can be removed, the wearer has to acknowledge rather than deny their presence.

I hope by providing the 'Jack Levy life story' I have displayed the necessary evidence to prove that a clutter-free mind is able to see things in ways preconditioned minds cannot.

When I talk about "clutter", I refer to the unwitting, best-intentioned one-sided grooming by those who themselves have been subjected to the same blind convictions. The restrictive, traditional mind-processing that I was so fortunate in not being subjected to.

Another observation was the way in which such stringent preconceptions and all the ritualised agendas they gave rise to, applied to whatever faith or religious belief happened to be followed by any of the doctrinal households that I visited. They were all, in effect, the same, but with different focus-points and statues, pictures and ornaments as if to prove it! Each household's specific beliefs would be referred to as the only "right" road, with the adults' directions and examples being those to emulate.

I noticed that individual 'captive' followings all around the world flourished in their own certitude. But I also asked myself if this was not a case of blindly following the leader rather than questioning whether they were the right leader to follow In the light of progress and new discoveries, it was also worth questioning whether the leader was the most up to date.

Some readers might take exception to the suggestion they are "blinkered". The perception of childhood conditioning might also be thought unfair or prejudiced, so I will vindicate one or two points which could help make a few of the coming observations a little easier to accept.

For a claim to have any significance, surely it should be able to stand up to the test of intelligent, informed scrutiny? It is the morality of this psychological block that needs to be questioned, as does the principle of never conceding that one might have been misinformed. It is a requirement of justice that any disputed issue needs to be put into the views of both sides, before any self-respecting judge (or sceptic) can soundly assess new information and treat the debate fairly.

This is the most serious problem which needs to be addressed, and this is no small obstacle! After all, admitting to having been subjected to direct or subliminal levels of thought-conditioning pressures throughout one's entire life is not easy. In fact, if one's belief is changed as a result of this book's arguments, the resulting turn-round could be really pivotal. It's the old case of closing your eyes when you don't like what you see. Now we're left with a crisis, and the only thing to do is open your eyes, acknowledge the result of our inaction and hope there's time to do something about it.

No less alarming is the conjecture that one's life might have taken a completely different route from the formative-years, conditioning-prevailed one being followed. This demonstrates the scale of the psychological mountain before us. An awful lot of serious realisation and mind-changing needs to be accomplished before we can hope to get ourselves organised. If we don't achieve this, then the all-too-obvious, grisly future is all that we and our offspring have to look forward to.

Chapter 25

Sensitive but Essential Observations

A little rationale applied to that which we're expected to unquestioningly accept

The realisation of my contemporaries' unwittingly being groomed became more and more conspicuous in my mind, and of more concern to me as I realised just how widely-spread was this blinkered-following of parental beliefs and traditions. My own opinions' dissimilarity to those around me became more of an issue in my life. My own, unfettered standing began to kindle a curious interest into just why I seemed to be alone in what was, to me, a logical viewpoint on religion and religious practises in general. Also why, to be specific, so many of the others had such strong and single-minded commitments to their own faith, whichever one it happened to be!

It was the unyielding inflexibility of believers that initially aroused one of the biggest causes of controversy. However, it was this same intransigence and the self-assumed 'superiority' of every religion which put them all into an easily-seen perspective and virtually resolved the issue for me. Pragmatically thinking outside the cage I could see how the early conditioning was universally applied, and how the integrity of each faith gradually crystallised into the inflexibility of devotion.

Being swept along by both convention and conformity, there was no real need for novices to debate the religious principle during this influential formative period. By the time maturity hardened an individual's opinions and ambitions, the background had been irrevocably set. Accepting that "certain matters are above being questioned", or that "it is a sin to do so" might sound illogical to the mature adult in today's advancing world. At the time it was different, but the situation is changing. Think back to your own childhood for a few moments. Don't you recall making a perfectly innocent observation or two that was just frowned on silently by those 'who knew better'? Or if for some reason you didn't want to go to church, a scolding was on the cards. You were always expected to "doff your hat" and show almost-royal humility in front of the vicar or other clerics? All of these and other subconsciously-integrated benchmarks served to set the implied subservience to religion and religious principles again, whichever faith happened to apply.

But the issue that really hit home to me was how indelibly-ingrained those formative years teachings grew to become on personal psyches. The reluctance to even listen to alternative views seemed to harden, even anaesthetise, as his my realisation and analytical questioning made these principles less credible to me. It was almost as if people's eyes were clenching even tighter.

Stand back and take an unprejudiced look at the religious tales you might have been expected to regard as factual, tales like Adam and Eve and Noah's Ark, or that it took seven days to create the world. All these anomalies and many more are known and accepted even among fervent believers to be fallacious, so where does "mistaken belief" stop and "load of poppycock" take over? How long will it take for the penny to finally drop? As our learning and knowledge increases with time, and more of these tales are discredited, then absolutely none of these scriptures can remain above sensible scrutiny.

As for their origin, let's have a brief and more informed look at the situation. It is undeniable that these stories are nothing more than fairy tales contrived to settle a society hungry for answers, despite their lack of soundness and inconsistencies. A more psychological insight into this might be called for. It concerns other issues of absolutely trifling significance which can have quite serious effects on even an intelligent person's life or psyche. It's, again, about those unrealistic phobias that can be seen all around us and, at risk of broaching a subject that can send a shudder through more people that would like to admit it, isn't it really bewildering how many instances there are of grown and intelligent men refusing to go anywhere near an absolutely harmless spider? Or people who jump up onto a chair because there might be a mouse on the floor? Or a cockroach, beetle, or other harmless creature?

But why should this be? It's not a fear that the creature might bite, as people may try to convince themselves, but for a psychological reason. An instant panic at the sight of an inoffensive creature may well be the result of a long-forgotten childhood shock. Seeing a parent in obvious panic mode cannot fail to influence a child in its formative years. Witnessing an adult in distress is a shocking and influential imprint. The incident is usually forgotten in time, but its impact has been firmly engraved. This makes it all too clear how such phobias can be passed on to the next generation! After all, how can an infant possibly know that its parents' phobias are unfounded? It takes the aptitude of unprejudiced reasoning to work that out, but the precedents set by terrified adults are the ones which embed themselves maybe deep into the psyche or personality of the child! The memory might fade but the reaction doesn't. This is precisely why evolution itself has hard-wired the formative years' unquestioning acceptance of teachings into us. Without yet having the mental capacity to know better, then we look and learn from our elders. In short, this is an example of imprinting, which takes place during those early and -impressionable, programmed-in parts of our lives. It's neither expected nor "done" for a child to ask "why?" if told or if witnessing something that might surprise them. In any case, at that early time in life, it's all new and there's no reason to question anything! Silent observation and soaking up of information is the norm for kids, and most of the incidents that provide this information slowly become a fading memory. So, thinking about this 'formative' time logically, is it not plain to see how fears and phobias become fixed? <u>Equally, this same fixture applies to those religious beliefs that are so relentlessly impressed from all directions</u>. They become immovably fixed with the passage of time, even over-ruling common sense when maturity eventually gets the opportunity to assert itself.

If the above thesis can be acknowledged, then it should clearly exemplify and explain the indelibility-factor of such entrenchment and, how this doesn't only apply to things like phobias. This illustration is intended to explain quite graphically, how fixed and virtually undeletable are the communicated or demonstrated perceptions taken aboard at this particular time in our lives. The same lack of logic applies to these phobias as it does to the fixation of religious beliefs embedded at this time of our lives.

Although these beliefs may have been passed on with good intentions, sound motives don't make sound information. Knowledge advances and, if we don't advance with it then we become out of date.

There has to come a time in life when the facts provided by maturity and new revelations might conflict with the facts told to us in our childhood. If this happens to discredit historical understandings and replace them with new ideas with evidence to support them, then surely we are better educated as a result? It is an obvious fact of life that our knowledge increases with advancing time and discoveries, so it is common sense to periodically have a look at all the fresh evidence and re-think our beliefs accordingly. This is a prime essential for any advance in sophisticated deduction and education.

In any case, such a periodic look at fresh evidence might actually endorse or reinforce any former belief. One cannot tell without reviewing it all. In the circumstances where it doesn't, would anyone want to go through his or her life under a crucial misconception simply because of the changes that the new knowledge or enlightenment might embrace? That, after all, is what education is all about, and not one of us should be above accepting new information as it evolves.

A particularly poignant question which demands to be asked is "at what point does steadfastness become nothing more than stubborn blindness"?

Chapter 26

Now for Some Really Uncomfortable Reasoning

Some facts about life that we ignore at our peril!

It might have been boring, but I hope this book has at least been circumspect and understandable. However, the composition has presented a challenge, in that I have spent a lot of time trying to both describe the basic origins of my open-minded outlook on life, and then to explain how this unusual viewpoint evolved into a detached way of seeing all the traditionally unquestioned understandings that prevailed around me. Some of these might have been trivial, but there were many which escalated into life-affecting importance.

I needed to promote my observations subjectively. However, in making a point about the dissimilarity of my opinions by using the principle of modern logic, the views I offered to less than enthusiastic ears were just too disturbing for some faithful traditionalists to even consider. I often found myself defending that which I thought to be decisive rationality against an intransigent argument of "I <u>know</u> otherwise." There is not a lot that can be politely said against that! (This demonstrates a similar mindless obstinacy to the response of quite a few people to the overpopulation crisis.)

This brings us to a mandatory issue which has been tentatively approached earlier. As it is of such contention, I thought it best to avoid instinctive rejection reactions by first introducing a few of its side effects. However, now these ancillary subjects have been covered, the bull can be taken by the horns. It is time to have a really close and survey of this over-protected subject. The name of this parody? Religion!

The more convincing the non-compliant arguments happened to be, the bigger the threat they presented. In order to discourage non-accordant, politically upsetting disturbances, the church practiced violent suppression. In the days when "witches" were burned for their opinions, when murder was rife and life was cheap, then discussing logic was a very dangerous thing to do! As a result of this 'discipline' through the centuries, the general infallibility of religions has hardened into the religious intransience we can still see now.

However, the inception of religion-challenging scientific discoveries began to weaken this self-legitimising delusion. Alternative conjectures with evidence to authenticate them arrived. But after such a long time enjoying immunity from questioning, and "fire and brimstone" ethics still carrying weight even today, it isn't surprising that it is taking a while to shake off the shackles of traditional belief.

It might be said, bearing in mind all the inconsistencies and lack of evidence, that in an unbiased climate any religiously-stated "fact" should sensibly be redefined as an "uncorroborated uncertainty". Because that is what they all are...

I understand that a believer may be ill at ease with this thesis, but there is the consolation of keeping one's own sound judgement in line with modern progress. Sound, logical rationalisation can change some deeply-ingrained opinions. Of course, the acceptance of reality over tradition is no mean achievement. It takes a considerable amount of integrity to concede that lifelong beliefs might be misconceptions!

It might be of comfort to know that the reality of a controversial and disagreeable conjecture has been opened for a sensible and unbiased investigation of its validity. It has been properly assessed and considered in an impartial fashion.

I close this chapter with a thought to ponder. Is not a deduction that has been drawn from free-thinking and open access from both sides of any argument, in reality, the only honest and valid one?

Chapter 27

After the Rationalisation, Some Logical Thinking

The application of basic, unprejudiced common sense

The previous chapter provided an insight into how the entire discipline of religion might have fostered a certain degree of immunity from criticism or examination. Before any decisions about the subject can righteously be reached, a prejudice-free deliberation is essential.

My next argument looks at all the facts, but has to climb a very steep hill against the blockade of conventionalism.

Why is it that an investigation into religion is more difficult than any other issue? The best explanation is psychology. Nobody likes to admit that the precepts by which their life is governed may not be true. Such an admission is not easy for anyone to make. It also exemplifies the scale of reluctance which has made this book so difficult to write, as it openly confronts the complacency of tradition. The above assertion serves to underscore the essential importance of a proper investigation into religion. It should be put into its true perspective for ethical reasons, before millions more are misled It is also dangerous for religious authorities to express any doubts. They are highly unlikely to throw their careers away by mentioning it.

So, we've had a look at the way beliefs are handed on and become consolidated with the passage of time and generations. We have weighed up the notion that for any precept to be considered as being sound then it has to openly stand up to any arguments and alternative theories in its own right. We have introduced the possibility that the narratives in holy texts might not all be quite true. Like Charles Darwin's theories, it may take decades before obstinacy towards change dwindles away and a logical understanding of religion becomes the norm It will no longer be a rigid and unarguable discipline, but a valuable part of our rich history.

It might not take all that long to materialise in today's world. We are now so much more receptive to new knowledge. The days of physical persecution are receding in more civilised nations, so it's only traditional stubbornness which still needs to be overcome.

Chapter 28

Atrocities, Mythology and Sanity Equated

A realistic vision into how today's 'faith'-murders evolved from simple naivety

Although the foregoing arguments are controversial, I hope that their doubts about traditional beliefs and ethics have awakened the reader to uncertainties which still need to be answered. Self-regard and the wish for further education might be influential too.

This chapter discusses the historical basis of religious beliefs with the atrocities which are justified in their name. Think of the Crusades, or the Spanish Conquistadores in South America. Those were often robbery, pillage and slaughter in the name of spreading the faith. There is a common factor to these outrages. The justifiers of them were conveniently out of reach, with only the word of an intermediary to pass on holy instruction to the perpetrators. As such, it was very easy to exploit greed and theft in the name of an imaginary authority. Gullible minions, persuaded to do the dirty work, fought and plundered in order to bring home the spoils of their conquests to swell the coffers of the church.

We only need hazard an informed guess about how many aeons ago man's belief in a god became an idea which evolved into such a paramount and fundamental entity in man's development.

Speech, or a responsive dialogue, would have been an essential medium for thought to be transmitted. It would probably not have been all that long after language had reached a level to allow inquisitorial intercourse. It would only then have been possible to start thinking seriously about "how" and "why". If the geologists' skull-profile/brain-section calculations and estimates and bone-conformity studies are correct, then it seems it might have been sometime between 1 and 1.8 million years ago that the very first, albeit primitive verbal (or meaningful noises, perhaps) communication was put into positive use. It takes more than a few grunts to hold a constructive debate and language as such would likely have taken up to half of that time to have achieved that level and to become a workable asset. Which would provide a (very rough) estimate of about half-million years or so ago when the "How?" and "Why?" questions were first seriously discussed. When they'd have pondered together and passed on their thoughts about the obvious questions like "How did we come to be?", "Where did all of those animals and plants that we eat, and depend upon, where did they all come from?", or "What about the water that we drink, the rivers, the sky above, the weather that can change so quickly and that affects us so devastatingly sometimes?" (or words to that effect) and, as we still do, "What's it really all about?"

They would have almost automatically progressed in their search for answers along the only path which their limited knowledge made available to them. It needed to provide them with them with satisfactory answers to all their questions, without any fear of supportable disagreement. The minds of the time were completely unaware of the principal of evolution. As far as they were concerned, everything had always been as it was, which led them to question who put it all there. What conclusion other than the obvious one could they have drawn? If it all was "put here in the first place", then someone or something had to have consciously "put it here". From there, "someone or something" presented the next big question, "who?" or "what?" It couldn't have been a "what" because objects cannot create anything. There was no alternative, it had to be a "who". Which, logically, led to the God answer – an Almighty being who provided all the answers to otherwise unanswerable questions.

Although some readers might like to think that the human race evolved from anthropoid primates fully aware about the sex/pregnancy/birth sequence, this is a somewhat unrealistic view.

The developing human mind would only gradually have associated the routine of sex with the later signs of pregnancy. Associating sex with reproduction might not have been as obvious as we like to think. It would have been easier to think of birth as another of those matters decided by the gods. Our ancestors had worked out an answer to their conundrum about the start of life, but this still left an unanswered gap about the matter of growing communities and what they had grown from.

Origins. Early man would have noticed within the timescale of his own life that his group or society enlarged with the passage of time. His elders would have told him that the size of their own community had been appreciably smaller. Inevitably those elders would have told of there being even less people in times long gone and they, in their own time, of even smaller numbers. You can probably see how this "Unanswered Questions" logic is developing.

In fact, it is just a systematic sequence. The conclusions our predecessors drew were the only realistic, answers to so many questions. The God-answer provided the overall solution, but the "numbers" enigma needed a little working-out. So, reversing the 'more-people-with-passing-time' observation above, it would have been natural for our ancestors at that time to have extrapolated this expansion backwards to the 'less-people/earlier-time' conclusion, which ultimately provided the very compatible "Christian-style" Adam and Eve concept. The next step is to co-ordinate time with religion. If it can be agreed that religion came into being not long after the power of meaningful dialogue came into man's life, then it was at least half a million years ago that both these features made their impacts in man's life. With the minimum of 500,000 years of the naturally-derived and reassuring theory of our creation, and with the ensuing homage, subservience and accountability to one or other form of god-figure, at least 25,000 generations would have been active in the relay of all teaching. Along with this basic instruction, the idea of sin evolved. Any lack of social acquiescence would be equated with sin, and we can only imagine how the human tendency to elaborate affected religious teachings over 25,000 generations.

Examining religious evolution situation from an impartial standpoint, is it not simply incredible that there are still some individuals who have difficulty putting ancient beliefs into their proper perspective? This is evidence of indoctrination's impregnability.

The creator figure evolved into providing the complete answer to otherwise unanswerable questions, and its early veneration has crystallised into the worship we see all around us today.

The passage of time meant the hardening of beliefs through each generation. The tales that were related faded into the distant and romantic past, blurring into the mystic unreality we identify with now. Innumerable people faithfully travel to their respective place of worship each week. All of them are quite intelligent enough to see the gradual but undeniable erosion of viability in the stories related to their religions, which they are expected to believe. They can also see that there is no factual or provable evidence that hours of singing, chanting or praying together has any positive benefit, and yet it still continues. It is a form of insurance. The believer as client pays a regular premium by making the effort to go, sitting humbly in a pew among other clients, saying all the right things on cue and contributing to the collection-box when it comes round. Very often there are other church-supporting activities and contributions are made accordingly. The insurance cover is that you qualify for an interview for the afterlife. If there's no afterlife, then you won't know anything about it, so nothing is lost. The price for the cover is little more than making the regular effort of getting there, and enjoying the social aspect.

It isn't a bad business for the Insurance Company. The value of all the proceeds is reflected in the elaborate and richly-bedecked houses of worship (and even the smaller churches have considerable collateral value). Some of the staff also seem to live fairly ostentatious lives.

It might be a sign of the times that in less credulous parts of the world, religion is slowly losing its validity. Religious observance in poorer and more fragile economies might still be fervent, but in the more secure sections of the world church-going is becoming no more than a social ritual. There is evidence of this in the shrinking congregations and the many deserted churches and chapels around the country. The worldwide occurrence of these observations proves it to be more than just a coincidence. Observation, education and the subsequent application of common sense is slowly prevailing over traditional intransigence. That's progress.

Many people might have observed the diminishing congregation numbers but nobody seems to deduce any meaning from it. With such an obvious indication, I would have thought the verdict was clear? The only time that our own churches can boast full pews is either when there is a very special occasion and/or when film crews are in attendance. Could there be a connection?

It is inevitable that there will probably always be hardcore attendees. There are the elderly, who regard their visits and donations as the insurance cover mentioned earlier, and there are those who enjoy the social aspect. So, it has to be conceded that church-going still has a value to some.

Chapter 29

What about the reliability of those ancient records?

An insight into the soundness of records upon which fixations emerge and flourish

The bases upon which all the 'popular' religions depend for their integrity are their sacred texts. Those need to be reviewed through eyes which have not been pre-conditioned, if the deductions are to have any value whatsoever.

Realistic analyses show most religious texts to be implausible. They also raise questions about the subsequent transferral of the message being conveyed. Perhaps the addition of a condition explaining that the scriptures describe events they say happened rather than stating that the events have happened, would be a more moral way of retaining the story. However, the purpose of telling the story in the first place is to convey what the teller thinks is factual. He thinks it is true because that's what he's been told by people that he trusts to be virtuous, honest and unbiased.

Then there's the 'permanence-factor', no printing-presses then, only one-off parchments to spread the stories at the time. Without widespread literacy, broadcasting was verbal. It is difficult to believe that the oral dissemination of texts maintained accuracy, and indeed whether the text themselves had been rewritten to suit contemporary politics. It needs to be remembered, that when such scriptures were compiled, the writers who did this were the monks of the time, and they had the bias of their own fervent belief to, let's say, 'make the story as pro-religion as possible. What about the situation with the New Testament? Not just decades, but (according to who you happen to believe), various historical records put down the "permanent" writings as being between fifty and a hundred and fifty years after the described events, so just how reliable is that? We all know how any story can be distorted by gossip from one end of a road to the other, so why should any of these chronicles be any less prone to natural-embellishment than normal gossip?

Think about the crowning incongruity. How, in the name of moral correctness, can these scriptures and stories which so many believe in possibly still carry any authenticity whatsoever? Even the eventual rendering of them to parchment doesn't make them immune from any falsification for political reasons! It is historically recorded that some texts have been doctored in this way, so how many more have been revised <u>surreptitiously</u> by those in power for their own benefit?

Is it not an insult to our intelligence that educated people are expected to listen to and swallow these tales as if they were today's news? If some tales can be put into a realistic perspective by asking a few questions, what about the rest of the rituals that are enacted on the same bases?

In order to set a constructive precedent, we have to look at both sides of the picture. Religion has provided us with a number of positives. The belief in an almighty authority and the culture engendered by that ideology has served to play a huge part in socialisation, moral ethics, legal standards and principles, seniority-rankings and so on. All of these administrations were in need of proper marshalling. When awkward questions that could possibly inflame pivotal dissent needed to be quelled, and when social standards and protocol had to be established, religion achieved all of that! In fact, it's hard to think how else we could have achieved this level of fraternity. However, time has moved on. We now <u>have</u> civilised standards, social integrity and, even more importantly to our future, we have our verified answers and logical alternatives to the only feasible beliefs that filled-in the unanswered questions of the time! So isn't it a recognisable fact that we've now reached a point in our evolution where we can move on to the next stage? We have reached that degree of perceptiveness and acumen where we can stand back and consciously appreciate that which faith has provided us with. We can see in retrospect how faith has served us, but today's knowledge can release it all, putting it into the new perspective as part of our rich and productive history.

With our ability to discerningly put outdated beliefs into their proper time-related context, we are advanced enough to understand the prevailing situation. We have constructively respected religion for so long, and it has served us well in providing us with answers and morals at a time when they were most needed. We have reached the pivotal point where we can positively affirm this to have been nothing less than an essential part of humanity's history. It must be recognised as such if we aren't to relegate ourselves to the level of those who still think that the earth is flat.

Naturally some might be reluctant to concede the unfolding realities in their new light but it is be the epitome of imprudence not to seek new answers when the old ones have so obviously run their course! It is our own prerogative if we wish to continue keeping our eyes tightly closed to all the advancements in our knowledge simply because it might contradict and put old beliefs into a new frame of reference. That is self defeating. We have to be free from the shackling complacency that is prescribed by hanging on to old beliefs if we are to be in a position to seek new knowledge. If we tell ourselves that we already know the answers, we are actively obstructing ourselves from new learning, or education.

Regarding any belief's implantation and retention, one cannot overlook the intensely subliminal effect that the semi-hypnotic, mass-participation of crowds can have upon people. The sheer power of this influence might not be realised by some, particularly in the context of this book, but it isn't difficult to expound. For example, music festivals and football matches, or political rallies and demonstrations. It can escalate and self-generate into anything from almost orgasmic pleasure to sadistic hate and wickedness.

Sometimes there's a charismatic character or group that can incite this emotion, but sometimes it's like a spontaneous fever that self-kindles and snowballs into almost-uncontrollable violence. That's how mass-meetings and mass-focussing work.

This also shows how totalitarian figureheads, anti-government or union leaders, charismatic presidents or revolutionaries can exploit all of this immense latent power for their own cause. It's almost like a form of mesmerism.

So why should personal appeal be any less influential on the masses just because it happens to be brought into effect in a church?

The only difference is that the speaker usually has the not-insignificant advantage of the inherent magnificence of the building, and the flamboyance of all the ostentatious symbolic images encrusted with gold and jewellery, candles, incense, drapes and adornments, to centralise the focus upon anything that he says. This all adds to the mesmerising appeal and addiction-effect of this ritualised sacrament. In addition, there is the hypnotic effect of mass participation which can raise such emotion. All these special effects have an intense subliminal outcome.

The sole object of this section is to put the fundamentals into perspective for the reader to analyse. It illustrates the way the facts of life are concealed whilst creating complacency, self-contentment and virtuousness, and tries to illustrate how this image materially holds back any attempt at discovery. Another object is to show how the bases of beliefs defy their authenticity, and presents my conclusions for the reader to personally assess from a new and, I hope, welcome viewpoint. The concluding opinion will be the reader's own verdict, weighed-up after seeing matters through newly-opened eyes.

Whilst on the subject of mass-influence, though, we come to the issue of terrorism.

If it can be accepted that influences from ideologies and beliefs can subliminally affect the direction of life itself, then is it not perfectly feasible that such mesmeric influences can be actively focussed on vulnerable, resentful, discontented people who are struggling through their lives with nothing materially to lose?

I refer to the growing scourge of terrorism and the psychology of its perpetrators. It is a sickness with terminal potential. From the time we can first react to that we see going on around us, right through adolescence and sometimes after that, we are naturally programmed to take that which our still-developing brains perceive as example-by-seniority, i.e. to do what we see our elders doing and follow their instructions without question. The evolutionary principle soon eradicated genes which didn't conform to this formula. It isn't only the intensity of this "learning" which needs to be appreciated, it's also the sheer persistence of all that which becomes ingrained during this period. That inbuilt barrier's depth is the first issue that needs to be accepted before the rest of this chapter will make sense.

If a child grows up to become a disillusioned young adult in an overcrowded world without any opportunities for work, without any future to look forward to, with a partner and multiple offspring to support, and with news-images of state-supported westerners with deep pockets and short arms mouthing their discontent whilst throwing away more food and goods than this poor, disenchanted young person has ever seen, then is it not inevitable that the only source of comfort, namely his church, becomes a vital part of his life? Then, if the elder at his place of worship tells him that he has "been chosen" to do any deed that will ensure he and his family's place in the next world, what's to be lost? If it's true, then his miserable life is exchanged for a wonderful afterlife. If it's not true, he'll know nothing about it anyway! So, who gains from any targeted massacre? The church, of course, and that is reflected in attendance and financial returns.

I have enormously reduced this to essentials, but there are a great number of disillusioned youngsters who would be typified by this picture. This is a perfectly feasible scenario for what lies ahead of us. Where desperate but naïve worshippers, seeking any form of solace, are subjected to this sort of 'grooming', told they have been selected to undertake suicidal atrocities for some cause's benefit and in return, will achieve a level of "greatness", worldwide publicity and a wonderful afterlife. This sounds a bit accusative to educated ears, but some are <u>that</u> desperate. It is a double exploitation of faith and hardship by those whose spiritual standing implies they ought to know better.

I have said enough for now about mass hysteria, exploitation and pseudo-divine coercion. It is a difficult and sensitive subject which needs to be tackled in small doses, so I will come back to it later.

Chapter 30

Informed Reasoning, or Comforting Fabrications from the Mists of Ancient History?

Conceptual analyses and conclusions

I return now to the matter of religious origins and the prehistoric circumstances that existed when communities were widely-dispersed. These societies would have evolved their own form of speech as they independently progressed and advanced their levels of capability, and with it their own lines of thought regarding the creation question and its answers. Whatever other ideas might have been considered, it is really only the logically derived and all-answering father-figure that we're all familiar with that could possibly have stood unchallengeable at that time and in those circumstances. Which would then have evolved, as suggested earlier, through any of its various depictions to become the basic, predictably-featured and pictured god-image that is common to all the diverse convictions and doctrines that developed within all of the different population-groups.

Regarding the pictorial point of view, whilst some communities would have depicted their all-answering creator in an imposing, fatherly human form, there would have been others with more-dependence on their different food-sources that might have dedicated their own creator-figure to portray this association, hence the variety of gods of the sea, or sun, or of rain or wind. Others might have identified their own creator with any of the wealth of other wonders that must have bewildered them; i.e. that encompassed stars and planets later in evolution as they became aware of them.

Whatever the choice of image, all the gods had one factor in common: their impeccability. No matter which society or god, the idolatry and worship which reflected the extent of awe, wonder and thanksgiving as it developed, it was all directed to devotion of a figure that was only communicable in the minds of the worshippers. It is an unavoidable reality that as communities flourished, the only way to manifest their gratitude would be in the form of conspicuous devotion to their invisible creator. This would have been displayed in prayer, praise, financial, artistic or physical offerings, as it is now.

The relevance of these psychological aspects needs to be emphasised, because the principle of how the system perpetuates has to be exposed. Consider the donated, expensive and elaborate decorative or enhancing artefacts, the collected or submitted riches, the labour and the tasks, provisions and gratuities, in fact everything that is done or donated by either the community as a whole or by any individual in the name or cause of any god or church. This serves to illustrate the means by which virtually all of the religious centres are able to flaunt such magnificence in their buildings and effects. Perhaps this is a profane observation, but it's a good example of commercialism at work.

First question; how many of the 'popular' churches are struggling to make ends meet? No answer? Where do they obtain all of their assets, wealth, resources, unimaginable property and acreage-worth of collateral, or all those ostentatiously-displayed ritual gowns, hats, sceptres and suchlike regalia, all loaded with jewellery and gold? Does it come from the congregation?

The next question is why do congregations feel the need to contribute to their religious centre's funds in this way? What return do they get for their donations? What is it that their church provides that they would be prepared to donate their last penny for? Just what is it that churches alone are able to provide? Apart from the social aspect, could it be the inferred contact or communication line with a god who can make life better?

So where is the evidence that these promises have any credibility? Who makes these unsustainable and phantom promises? Could it be none other than the foundation (or its representatives or agents) that has everything to gain by the stories and promises being swallowed by an easily-taken-in audience? Viewing the situation from a businesslike aspect, would it really be too callous to suggest that the church really is nothing but a successful business which trades by using unsustainable pledges. The consumer, of course, does not know this.

The previous paragraph might have presented a very unpalatable line of thought for many readers but please think about why this is so. If my allegations were unreasonable or implausible then there would be nothing of substance to worry about. , However, if they have provided fresh questions or presented solid contentions, then common sense demands further study.

After all, an analysed revision of opinion is an <u>advancement</u> of knowledge.

Let's return to the psychology behind church attendance. In the beginning, the god-answer resolved imponderables. It positively provided not only answers to the questions about life and its origins, but also gave a meritorious focus-point for the thanksgiving need. It provided an anticipation that made the uncomfortable inevitability of death a little less foreboding and provided a personal-accountability consideration which set an ethical standard for the new communities. It gave an implied virtuosity or indemnity for its followers, and there were many other reasons which made church-going and worship an advantageous practice. In pre-historic times, the trickle of followers naturally increased as the above psychological and social benefits attracted people. When the harvests or the hunting and fishing yields were plentiful for the worshippers, then the thanksgiving culture would be happily applied, particularly ardently in hope of earning the subsequent season's fruitful returns. Everybody was happy and the worshipping became more sincere because of it. It is ironic that in times of bad fortune, calamity would be explained away as a justified punishment for an inadequate display of gratitude or humility. From the faith's point of view, it was certainly a win-win situation. The creation and the expansion of this win/win state of affairs for the god-culture simply could not fail. As more and more of the community saw what they were told was the "evidence", in conjunction with the bonding pressures of the relevant society, any outsiders eventually would have been persuaded to join in, and the faith's following strengthened accordingly.

The accumulated worship, social and communal self-support, and the all-important togetherness of the belief's followers and worshippers made it quite natural that faith was the heart of the community. In addition, all of this communal spirit self-generates the passion of such belief and devotion, so that anyone with social standing in the locality would feel an implied need to voluntarily and visibly ply his personal energy or other form of donation to the benefit of the church. As more people paid this sort of homage and glorified the society's particular god, this would apply a not-so-subliminal pressure on any which didn't. It was a case of join the believers or be an outsider. So we can see how belief flourished.

The very strength of this unanimity would very firmly discourage any dispute of the fundamentals of that specific culture. Whether or not anyone had any doubts or suspicions, they were better off not expressing them. If any scepticism were even to be whispered about, it would mean one person questioning the integrity of an entire community.

That might be alright if the belief were well-founded and plausible, but if there were any suggestion that the entire community was taking it aboard as a matter of convenience, then the person speaking out would present a danger to the community and be silenced. At that time, of course, there wasn't any other believable alternative, so it was a case of that belief or no belief!

The above depiction of establishment and self-security of faiths is offered as a well-reasoned and cogent alternative to traditional beliefs about the origin and establishment of religions. It also puts into perspective the ways and reasons that they flourished as they did.

There's another associated factor to be considered too, and that's the issue of the combined effects of psychological influences. Coercion and persuasion, even intimidation, goaded outsiders to comply with the community, while existing believers perpetuated the faith.

I hope that the reader has been offered a refreshing new aspect on the current state of a changing situation, but also on the weakness of the foundations which aeons-old beliefs are based on. By directly contesting traditional dogmas, my views present, substantiate and rationalise the evidence so readers can judge for themselves.

If the dispute of ordained beliefs is justifiable and well-grounded, then it will not be difficult to concede how the intensity and depth of glorification consolidated itself into its current level of obduracy, even when today's evidenced discoveries reveal that progressively more of the foundations upon which this teaching rests are proved to be unsound.

This chapter explains how quickly convenient beliefs would have escalated, quite naturally, into the many religious branches that were and still are so robustly and staunchly defended. Worship gradually assumed the rigid and socially important role we can see around us today. Nowadays, any parentally-emphasised continuity might become more desperate as youth-observed dissension stands up against it, but that may merely be a harbinger of the breakdown of the status quo.

Chapter 31

Time for a Realistic Look at Developments

The hardly-credible tales spawned by time-entrenched 'facts'

Perhaps enough has been written about the unsound basis of god-ethics in general. The next stage is to put the sub-divisions which have developed from them under the microscope.

Generally speaking, quite a high proportion of the scriptures seem to be based on nothing more substantial than recounted visions, or hallucinations. It is upon such tenuous beginnings that an inordinate amount of credence and belief is forged! Even in today's world, there are any number of conditions which can precipitate hallucinations, and poor hygiene is one of them. But think for a moment about life at those prehistoric, or even through to medieval, times. There were no supermarkets to provide carefully prepared and hygienically-wrapped food. Food included offal, sun-dried or salted meat and fish, sometimes long-stored and much-handled. People didn't wash their hands after defecation, and there was no toilet paper.

There were also berries, seeds, fungi, tubers and foliage which would have been collected to supplement meals, and often would have been eaten uncooked too. In addition, there were 'magic' mushrooms, berries and barks which could be taken for kicks in the same way they are now. Flies and airborne disease must have been widespread, so there is also contagion and infection to consider, and the effects of fever, epilepsy, lack of food or sleep, schizophrenia and intoxication. Any one of these conditions might have caused a hallucination, or a so-called holy vision. Who says it is a holy vision? Someone who's been under the effect of a drug, perhaps? If such figments of the imagination can happen all the time in today's world, it is certain that they could have happened earlier too. Can it really be even basic common sense to take these vision-inspired understandings or "holy messages" as being of any fidelity whatsoever? That doesn't only apply to visions that the afflicted person might have been aware about. It is a fact that some hallucinatory cases are completely unaware afterwards that they have been in a comatose condition. When they come round, they don't realise it, thinking that what they've 'seen' is all real! So, if that person happens to be the convincing or charismatic communicator that we mentioned earlier, one who can put his story over in such a way that it's believable to the usually-"welcoming" crowd , it's quite feasible that such things fostered the start of the scriptures' stories. It is not a completely unlikely scenario.

Think about the description of a "welcoming" crowd. Wouldn't they be in a position where they not merely wanted but needed to hear about wondrous things which provided them with all the answers to so many questions? Particularly if it was news delivered to a news-hungry audience in strenuous and fact-deprived times, Wouldn't they all-too-readily believe it? Afterwards, they would reinforce what they "wanted to hear" by worshipping the newly introduced focus of belief.

That is the way that human psychology works. If there's any doubt about that, look at some of the T.V. adverts selling goods with unrealistic claims!

Having achieved an unexpected element of fame, the originator of the 'vision' would be very happy to expound the story people wanted to hear. This is completely natural and psychologically typical, and the issue of elaboration of the basic tale is very pertinent. After all, it is quite natural for humans to subject facts to a little embellishment, if only to make their accounts a little more compelling, and thus more in demand. The sequence progresses predictably: the originator gains the self-esteem any extrovert craves, the audience hears about a wondrous episode which cannot be ignored, the community's centre of the budding religion gains valuable veneration (and increases its congregation-numbers), and everyone's a winner! The above is just the sort of thing which could have occurred. In all the world's simultaneously-expanding communities, would this not have been the situation that transpired time and time again, with variations? Any charismatic individual with the mystical drawing-power to make an impression could literally exploit this. Is this just a fanciful thesis, or an inevitable sequence which developed spontaneously as a result of hallucinogen-unaware and insanitary circumstances.

Whilst on the subject of elaboration, nearly everybody is inclined to exaggerate a story when they tell it, lying to impress listeners. Some might even be tempted to fabricate a story, which might in its turn be elaborated too.

Doesn't everyone know at least one person whose accounts need to be taken with a pinch of salt? So, why should it have been any different historically?

If the above can happen anywhere, then it can happen everywhere. This accounts for all different religions having different variations of 'the truth'.

When put into a realistic perspective, the implausibility of related stories quite seriously compromises a large percentage of sacred texts upon which so much of religion depends. Whilst on the subject of authenticity, it might be an opportune time to have a properly-balanced look at the Old Testament. It has a foundational essence in many base religions and derivative cults. Modern advances in disciplines such as technology, geology and astronomy are gradually challenging and disproving more and more texts which have historically been taken as factual? Most modern believers recognise and accept such inconsistencies, understanding that, historically, they were relevant. But why are they still viable today? Unaware minds still believe flimsily-fabricated tales because they are the only ones that closed minds can accept.

If we are aware that some tales have already been disproved, why should we not be equally aware this will probably happen to all the others? As technology advances, those upon which so many religions depend will be discredited. Such a logically-founded observation must put those testaments into a new light. For how much longer will any reliability in them continue to be stubbornly maintained?

Chapter 32

A Few More Actualities

The origin of 'magnificence' and how it promotes image

History relates of several major biblical re-writes. There might well be others that haven't been disclosed or discovered. Just because a tale has been printed in ink, chiselled on a stone face or imprinted on a clay tablet, this relative permanency does not somehow sublimely render the story or the message that it conveys to be a factual truth, as any newspaper magnate will confirm! That depends totally on the creator of the texts both being told the true facts, and not elaborating on them for material or psychological gain. There is nothing to prevent the texts or their disclosures being revised to accommodate the demands of changing politics and new priorities. It is not unlikely that the bureaucracy with the power and motivation to order these revisions would ensure it is done covertly.

The fact that a holy book is flaunted in the form of an impressive bound volume with gold-leaf impressions and ornamentation does nothing whatsoever to make the contents more authentic. This is equally true of the person reading them, parading himself on the rostrum dressed up in jewellery-laden flamboyant robes and headdresses, flourishing a jewel-encrusted mace. It is all in the interest of image and its implied fidelity.

Church-going folk will probably be well aware of the, disparities between their scriptures and the scientific/historical/geographical/astronomical discoveries, but it appears that a quiet deference is the popular order of the deity. That brings us to the next, blatant inconsistency, that of the immense, almost vulgar, amount of wealth that, as witnessed by all of the buildings' splendour and unnecessary embellishments. Why should all this ostentatious parading be necessary? Isn't the discipline itself of adequate grandeur? Doesn't all of this sequestration materially compromise the 'humble' ethics of the causes themselves? After all the expenses and running-costs of the system, surely all the rest of this wealth should be used for the benefit of the needy, believers or not, within the community? Can it be convincingly explained how the hoarding and flaunting of all this collateral wealth does anything to enhance the discipline, or the value of worship?

Even more questionable is the manner by which these doctrinal movements acquire their affluence. There are the relatively legitimate collection-returns, tithes, bequests and donations from well-meaning, faithful people who either willingly or under an implied-obligation, pay their expected dues. There are wealthy benefactors who like to display their generosity to the public around them, and those who like to keep it quiet, hoping their reward will come in due course. That, in itself, is a substantial income.

What about the unscrupulous and corrupt returns from "Holy wars", where self-righteous and religiously justified armies went on crusades to invade and occupy non-conformist lands, literally plundering whilst telling the innocent people who live there and who have their own beliefs and deities what they must believe in! How's that for democracy? There have not been many such invasions which haven't had a religious cause. The aggressors conveniently claim the righteousness of their cause as they kill and loot for their church or country's benefit, and into the vaults it all goes. Do the poor and needy of any faith ever see more than token hand outs towards their welfare? Is it not a typical scene to see the more-advantaged faithful do all the work and supply the hand outs for the needy in times of hardship? In other words, is it the church or the congregation that does all the work? Whichever it is, it is the image and name of the church which benefits from this charity.

This observation is a generalisation and is open to correction, but its purpose is to highlight the matter of assets and revenues balanced against the popular churches' help for the needy of their flock.

No disrespect whatsoever is intended towards charities and their staunch volunteers who work so hard to selflessly to raise all that they can in support of their church's benevolent cause. Perhaps this interpretation is mistaken, but it appears that the members of the charities who do all of the work and supply or attract all the necessary goods. However, all the credit gained is in the name of the church and thereby calls the important public-magnetising attention to it.

In case it isn't obvious, this criticism doesn't apply to smaller, often overstretched groups where religion is the cause, but wealth is unknown. Their supporters will be quite aware of their non-implication.

Chapter 33

A Few More Thoughts

Reviewing and placing into perspective some of the issues

Despite the fact that these illustrations and impressions about some of the main churches' ethics could imply otherwise, this is not an anti-church or anti-religions composition. Indeed, there is absolutely no intention to demean, devalue or discredit any church as an institution, or the basic principles upon which they are founded. As has been made clear earlier, from the consideration of the social aspects alone, it is felt that as we developed and needed the stabilising effects of civil standards, the majority of communities might well not have been able to flourish as they did without such a presence. The churches carried, and might still have, a truly irreplaceable part of any civilised society, very often being a nucleus about which the local communities evolved and developed (note the past tense!).

No, it is not the principle or the religious institutions themselves that are being focussed-on and questioned, but those who exploit the credo and moral standing that is analogous to the discipline of religious association. Those who capitalise-on and surreptitiously use the ethical prestige, taking advantage of it to extort or make for their own benefit or that of a syndicate, the maximum returns that can be squirrelled away. Sounds accusative? Just look at the affluence that they actually display in the churches and cathedrals, etc. Members of the churches' hierarchy want for nothing! They might make an occasional "gift", but overall gains from the resulting boost in image would probably show any such outlays as nothing less than speculative investment. That's how big business works. Some might not like to think about their much revered religions in such a basic way, but look at the situation from the overall outlay/income balance, at the immensity of the stockpiled assets and collateral, at the gaudy extravagance that's displayed at every opportunity, and take an investigative perusal at the psychological exploitation and manipulation of the way that the congregation's inbred homage-compliance is milked for all that can be. If that is not heartless and callous business, which benefits the church's administration and assets, what is it?

This is a prudent point to stand back and review the matters that have been raised so far, before the next stage is put forward for consideration.

First, it is quite probable that the wide-ranging and naturally-troubling subject of religious origins might be the biggest and most difficult standpoint for traditionalists to confront. They have been presented in a sensible and logical way which makes the rationalised contentions more than merely feasible, and hence worthy of serious thought. The thesis about the possible beginnings shows the consequential assumptions concerning the basic creator concept. I depict how countless generations of parent-child indoctrination has stabilised belief into the fixed and comfortable guise we see it in today.

I reviewed the way the aforementioned process progressively produced descendants who were less enquiring or open-minded about the implausibility of all the stories and beliefs that they were furnished with. In fact, it's only recently that the naivety of acceding to these tutorials has manifested itself sufficient to overcome the steadfastness (or stubbornness) of built-in beliefs. The growing doubts and willingness to forfeit fables in favour of intelligent logic mean that the inevitable showdown must soon come to a head.

I have put into a sensible and mature perspective the lack of viability of many basic stories upon which so many religious foundations are actually established. I have observed how many different, contradictory accounts are adhered to with equal immovability by their respective believers. This aspect in itself is offered as evidence of every belief's fatuousness as they stand!

Basic psychology can be exploited in order to instil allegiance to any religion, and we've seen who are the real financial winners and losers when it comes down to the big money fundamentals.

Now is the long overdue time for a rethink about your journey's new direction, which should surely be obvious to anyone with basic common sense and a logical mind.

If there should still be any stoic doubters about origins and subsequent developments, then think about this. It is a matter of fundamental importance to our destiny that our long-standing beliefs are evaluated for what they are and the part that they have played in our development. They should then be reclassified accordingly as nothing more than a part of humanity's history. There is nothing sinister or immoral in that. It is merely constructively observing facts as they are! Without the clutter of out dated indoctrinations, you can change your outlook from "auto mode" to "open-mindedness". Whenever any new and verifiable knowledge makes itself known, then it can be seen, assessed and accepted in an educational light, rather than immediately dismissed. That is one of the rudimentary elements of intelligence.

With advances in technology and science at our disposal and the new knowledge and acumen they provide, is it really possible to simply ignore all of the new knowledge in order to blindly follow that which you have been told by others who didn't know any better? It must be reviewed in the light of how the entire direction of one's life can be influenced and directed by the belief that has been instilled by this increasingly-discredited information. Is the disciplined reaction you've been trained to respond with just one huge barrier which actively prevents your seeing modern existence through modern eyes? Modern revelations are there to be seen. There is evidence to support them, but you have to have your eyes open to see it.

Religion has played an important, even essential, role in providing the growing civilisation with answers, social regulation and order, but, as its foundations gradually crumble away with new perceptions, then the religionist role can be consigned to the annals of our history. This is the same as the way we grow out of believing in Santa Clause. Maturity reveals the sham.

The importance of this analogy is examined in the next chapter.

When we think of holy wars, ethnic cleansing and the religious repressions in the Middle East, it is worth considering the following analogy. In the case of the religious discipline itself, there is a certain similarity with drug use. First, there is the placebo which does absolutely nothing, but the taker convinces himself that it does and thus feels better. Then there are hard drugs, which foster addiction, ruthlessness and an absence of value in the world around. Can you see an interesting parallel?

Chapter 34

Another Aspect

An analogy that illustrates how childhood's formative years are exploited

It's just possible that some might still think that something as crude and primitive as indoctrination could only apply to lesser mortals without much intelligence. Let's look at a correlation.

Remember when you were told as a child that a fat, laughing man with a huge white beard and a red fur-trimmed costume somehow managed to land his reindeer-drawn sled on the roof of your house? He clambered down the chimney with a sack full of presents for the children who had "behaved themselves throughout the year". When you woke up at the crack of dawn on Christmas morning, you'd excitedly find all those wonderful presents which seemed to be just what you really wanted! In conjunction with all the other gifts and special food, Christmas was a festivity on a par with birthdays. Was it a commemoration? That was what it was called.

Santa Claus was a huge and important part of Christmas when you were young. But how long was it before you put two and two together and worked out that Santa was a charade? It was nothing more than a myth which you'd been led to believe in by your trusted parents. In short, your own common sense put the fairy story into its true perspective. You fathomed out for yourself that it was a fruitful but otherwise pointless sort of game. You gradually came to see that it was really only for the benefit of the small, less aware children. It was the practical impossibility of what your parents had told you that really mattered.

We'll come back to the white lie issue a little later. When you'd reasoned out the fallacy and its rationale, did you come clean to your parents? Did you tell them that the story just didn't ring true and that Santa Claus couldn't possibly do and provide all the wonderful things that they said he could? That the Santa story was rubbish, in fact? Of course you didn't. You did what all children do and continued to enjoy the fun and exuberance of the masquerade. It would be a shame to spoil everyone else's fun and to cast a shadow over it all by telling anyone about the application of logic. How much more thoughtful (not to mention comfortable and rewarding) it would be just to let your parents carry on thinking of you in that starry-eyed way for as long as you thought that you could get away with it, or until conscience stepped in.

The colourful concept of the annual Santa Clause masquerade is an analogy which positively illustrates the way children's minds can be manipulated. It isn't even really manipulation: parents just stating a fact is adequate proof for children to adopt it. Children are not alert or developed enough to see the banality of the many impracticalities and the story is taken aboard without question! This illustrates how the formative years of childhood work. The Santa story is fun, but the analogy illustrates a more serious issue – that of formative assimilation. It teaches the rudiments of life, instils the basics of survival and locks into the mind anything about belief and religious rituals that their parents believe. Children are automatically conditioned to follow all and every example or instruction propounded by their elders. They just have no reason whatsoever, or experience of life, to question anything that is told to them by anyone on a senior level. All is taken on trust.

The second feature of this analogy concerns the gradual realisation that all is not quite as you've been told that it is. What you've been told differs from that which you've discovered and worked out for yourself. You have been misled, yes, but in the interest of your own fun and pleasure. Any white lies in such circumstances don't matter, but they are an example of early duplicity.

The Santa Clause analogy puts belief into an uncomfortable frame of reference. It draws a comparison between the way an originally-accepted story gradually becomes less credible with age, and those precepts about religion which have been drummed in and regularly practised since early childhood. Coercion is almost invariably applied in varying degrees of insistence. Regarding Santa Claus, it was more comfortable and rewarding to keep your doubts to yourself. That way, nobody had to confront anyone else with accusations about pretence and a comfortable status was established.

Everyone was a winner.

Let's examine the religious parallel. In both situations, stories and beliefs are presented as 'facts' to a child who has no alternative or reason to think otherwise. Both the Santa story and the religious beliefs have been set in place, but the Santa story becomes less credible with time, and there is a probably-subconscious decision to either let it be or let it go.

There are two parallel beliefs, both of which have been presented as facts and thoroughly endorsed by elders. Both have only hearsay to validate them. So, if we grow out of Santa as we discover it is fallacious, why does this not apply in exactly the same way to religious beliefs as they, too, become uncorroborated?

The discretionary continuation of the Santa masquerade could equally apply to its religious parallel. Sooner or later the breakdown of its authenticity and the rationalisation of its dodgy origins must over-rule the comfort of not admitting the delusion. The sooner this is put into perspective, the sooner we can look to the future with unblinkered eyes!

As children, we are all programmed to follow the examples our parents and mentors set us. That is the way that evolution works. If we didn't emulate our role models there is a fair chance that our survival as a race might have been prejudiced. The purpose of this chapter is to emphasise just how deeply and subliminally-ingrained, all of these imprinted impressions can unknowingly become as the passage of time moves from those formative years into adulthood. The Phobic reactions to harmless creatures serves to illustrate the irrational intensity of these impressions once they are established. The same pertinence applies to religious indoctrinations, even more so due to continuity, indisputable appositeness and eminence. This, again, is evidence of the barrier that free and open-minded thinking has to overcome before it can be applied.

When we were growing up our parents provided teaching and guidance with the best intentions. Unlike us, they were unaware of the knowledge eroding the basic ethics of religion. Even if they had doubts themselves, would they have been circumspect enough to advise their children about these thoughts that contradicted long-instilled scriptures?

Chapter 35

When does Blind Obstinacy become Mindlessness?

Some of the unbelievable things that 'intelligent' people still give credence to

This chapter updates and brings into focus several more assumed understandings. There are quite a few long-standing beliefs which are still taken at face value, even though their fundamentals are collapsing. There is a danger that they can influence acceptance of alternative, more authentic knowledge.

Allow me to explain. It was only a few generations ago that expressing disbelief was derided as a sin, particularly disbelief in fables like the genetically questionable Adam and Eve story, or Noah's Ark. How about the way the world was created in seven days? It is historically known that all of these narratives and more were taken on board by faithful believers at that time in our past when there simply were no other all- answering options available to the solution-hungry listeners! In short, it was a case of either believing the scriptures with the rest of society, or standing alone as an atheist with the life-imperilling prejudices that were inherent with non-conformity in those days.

Our new level of knowledge provides us with the choice of whether or not to accept new information. More and more religious tales are gradually being disproved, eroding the substance of their infallibility. Alternatively, people can choose to pretend that the invalidating evidence doesn't really carry any credibility. In centuries long past, belief was almost mandatory. There was a very strong social element, but the reason for the prevalence of faith was because it was unassailable. There was no reason to believe otherwise. And the implied threat of some sort of afterlife retribution carried no little weight in the situation too!

We have advanced since then. No longer can we blindly say that creation was a premeditated and conscious exploit by some all-powerful agency, and that it is a sin not to believe this, any more than we can definitely or authoritatively insist that no such medium started it all! The only thing that know for certain is that we don't know the answer. It is arrogance to consider any belief to be true belief. Those who practice that principle display blind stubbornness. Could it be that they have most to lose by others' release from their faith by logical, impartial thinking and enlightenment?

Things are so different now that even traditionalists have to concede that the tide of faith-challenging knowledge has swept our thinking about blind faith into a new dimension: feasibility. Religion has changed its role in our lives. No longer is it the "be-all and end-all that" it has been since the time when it was the only answer. The advent of new and completely discrediting knowledge has necessitated the impartial reassessment of religions' foundations, leading to obvious conclusions that put religion into the new category of being nothing more or less than a rich and crucial part of our history. Kierkegaard wrote: "There are two ways to be fooled. One is to believe what isn't true, the other is to refuse to believe what is true.", and Einstein wrote that "He who is aware that he doesn't know is a wiser man than he who thinks that he does know."

Nowadays the situation is so completely opposite that that belief is no longer intellectually credible without sensible analysis. Blind belief is thoughtless, demonstrating an unthinking unawareness of what's happening in the world around us.. But why should we assume that such blindness is confined to idiots? It might sound a little illogical for people to think in that blinkered way, but the power of doctrine and orthodoxy takes a lot of refutation. Look at those ostensibly intelligent people round the world who despite all of the conflicting evidence that is there before their eyes, adamantly and stubbornly believe that the Earth is only 6,500 years old, and others who think that it was created as an intact and running concern. Such instances serve to illustrate the existence and tenacity of some convictions that presumably normal and sensible people are capable of believing. What is in their minds is for anyone to guess!

It is hard for clear-thinking people to understand, perhaps, but these blindly evidence-defying contentions do actually flourish where people are able to talk themselves into believing whatever it is that they want to believe in. They stubbornly refuse to even consider looking at any conflicting but clear-cut evidence that is manifestly there in front of their eyes! They exist, though, and serve in this composition as living proof of the obstinacy that human beings can bring into action.

If a person or a group of persons doesn't want to accept that which is evident before them, that is their right! Some might say that their capacity for reasoning might be suspect, but their existence provides proof of how fatuously stubborn and deliberately unseeing human beings can be when they want to be. We can see around us how nature is capable of programming other creatures into managing to navigate thousands of miles above or below the sea's surface to within inches, so why should the element of relatively simple imprinting not apply to creatures like us?

Imprinted instincts are hard to fathom. We might never fully understand how such direction-finding criteria can be transmitted from one generation to another without any form of verbal, visual or guiding communication. Our own formative years mandates are relatively transparent, even ingenuous in comparison. Verbal religious indoctrination is simplicity itself. It is passed on without ever being put under any form of scrutiny. When the belief itself is shown to be founded on an unsound or unreliable premise, then moral correctness comes into the issue. Do <u>any</u> parents tell their children this "this might not be true but..."? It is easier to pretend that it's all the same as it was when they were children: that the stories are sound. All this is so that their comfort is not prejudiced. This all serves to bring into focus just one more aspect about depth and perception, but we'll come to the comparison of human and animal instincts and control in due course.

Chapter 36

We've Prepared the Stage, Now for the Dramatics

Put yourself into the shoes of Suicide bombers, Terrorists and Radicals.

Let's look at the equation in this way. Ingredient A is the deteriorating situation comprised of all the world's growing stresses. It can be seen around us in news reports and general discontent. Diminishing mineral and water resources, administrative fears about climate instability, financial breakdowns, social disruptions, political corruption and duplicity are being covertly subdued by those ministries which have an interest in concealing or minimising the cause and probably ultimate conclusion of it all. And overpopulation is the affliction which causes all these symptoms.

Overpopulation is the virtually unfettered and uncontrolled eruption of human beings into a world of very limited resources. Human beings have to be fed, watered, sheltered and gainfully employed. Nothing is being done about this approaching impasse. It's almost as if it were not important that this planet's capacity to support human life is limited. Just look around the world and see for yourself the news reports about malnourishment around the world, the people deprived of clean water, those who are scratching a meagre living from whatever can be dug up, caught or stolen? It's not just that we are reaching the maximum capacity of our agricultural productivity, but that the artificial nutrients on which it depends are also limited, and there are collateral penalties for using them. The water supply is not just becoming more difficult to find and sustain, but over-exploitation and river-damming is destroying downstream lands which depend on the water and its alluvial deposits. We can see this in the vast, new, uninhabitable dustbowls, deserts and salt-flats in so many lands. All forms of mineral resources are running out, demanding deeper drillings and mines which have limited success and collateral effects. There's continually increasing news about economy-failures (even in the 'richest' lands, it seems), the famines and droughts, and the corrupt totalitarian regimes around the world that exploit these weaknesses. But the real cause of all this anarchy is the fact that we won't recognise that we have a population crisis. By the time it is finally conceded, we won't be able to do much about it.

The government might try to suppress the evidence, but it cannot be avoided if you keep up to date with world news. Neither can the arithmetical certainty of the catastrophic quandary ahead of us!

The worldwide concealment of the coming deadlock is not only the epitome of ministerial irresponsibility, but a virtual signature on humanity's death warrant! Our politicians ought to know better. In fact, they probably do, but are too frightened to face the public reaction on hearing such disclosures. It is an impasse.

Let us look at Ingredient B in our equation. Imagine that you live in a part of the world where only a privileged minority are able to live in a relatively luxurious way, and the majority are only able to stay alive through hand to mouth means. I refer to those immense areas in China, India and Russia which together constitute a significant part of the world's population. There are possibly billions of people who are the victims of river-damming, aquifer-draining, air and water pollution effects and land-ravages through oil, mineral and timber abstraction and access. Imagine yourself in another, similar, situation where there is no work, no social benefit, no future even, and where the only solace is in worship where any little that you might have is invested in the hope of divine help. In these and many other cases around our deteriorating world, it is becoming so obvious that there simply is no future to look forward to. You and your family are cold and hungry as scarcities become more and more evident. There are dearer or fewer provisions to be shared, wealthier and/or more militant authorities make more demands as more imports need to be balanced by less produce, and greedy companies take mineral assets. The disparity between 'those who have' and 'those who don't' grows bigger.

In both Ingredient A and Ingredient B, 'those who have', by virtue of their very nature, or self-protection by suppression, or their growing awareness of the tenuousness of the position that they enjoy, ensure that "those who have not are" kept in line and are very well aware of their manifestly-flaunted prevalence. This is usually displayed by physical bullying in order to discourage any thoughts about defiance or rebellion. Not only would you be distressed about the deteriorating conditions, but you would also be very aware of flamboyant and overfed western societies shown on television, where everyone seems to have everything that they demand to excess. In that so-influential part of the same world, deep pockets, short arms and loud mouths predominate!

The next stage in our imagined survey is obvious. In that position, you would look at this unfairness and ask yourself why you and your family were starving while others enjoyed" having everything that they might wish for, more than they really need, in fact?" You have no chance of changing the way that things are, nor can you see any possible way of making life easier for you and your family. What other refuge is there? The only place which might possibly offer some form of comfort is your church, where you do the only thing that you still can do, which is to offer your deepest prayers in the desperate hope that a response might lead to a better life for you and your family! It would be the one remaining hope in your miserable life. You would certainly not be alone, either!

Looking circumspectly at the masses who find themselves in this predicament, we can connect the growth of disillusionment to the growth of terrorism Discontent with the inevitability of worsening conditions and the almost daily news reports about apparently religiously-provoked terrorist activity cannot just be coincidental? It cannot be claimed that the growing unrest, instability and civil discontent has no real connection with the increase in terrorism. So how is this orchestrated?

There are so many different churches or religious syndicates around the world and you could belong to any one of them. If the relevant ecclesiastical hierarchy was able to convince you that "forgiveness", "blessedness" or some other form of godly recognition awaited you and all of your dependants if you were to actively show your "love and devotion" by martyring yourself, making a willing sacrifice of your pitiful and inadequate life in the name of a particular deity, then it is likely that you'd at least be tempted. After all, you would certainly not be forfeiting a great life, and the very worst that could happen is that you'd know nothing about it afterwards.

All this might sound a little unlikely to the western reader, but it needs to be put into the context of the potential bomber. In less stable parts of the world, these are activists who have little to lose materially. They are unemployed and have an abundance of spare time on their hands to construct bombs. They are probably being convinced by their religious mentors that a paradise is awaiting their souls in gratitude for their magnificent sacrifice, and self-mitigating their murderous plans with prayers and meditation. These usually young and gullible individuals are successfully accomplishing their cult's ambitions to spread fear and terror with progressive attacks anywhere around the world. Nowhere is safe from them! The human race is producing more and more souls into a world that is running out of the means to support them! There is a flood of undernourished and easily-propagandised believers ready to do anything to improve their lot. These poor, desperate obsessives know that they'll die as martyrs, if nothing else. As faithful believers, however, they know that the cult that they've given their life for gains both in its worldwide recognition and its fear-boosted wealth! More terrorism means less stability, and less stability means more opportunities for the cult to exploit.

Ingredient A is comprised of the population heedlessly breeding more people into a world with less resources. Ingredient B embraces the world of the bitter, deprived and resentful beings who have only their religion to call on for whatever comfort they can glean. Ingredient A plus ingredient

B, the formula for terrorism. "Men never do evil so completely and cheerfully as when they do it from religious conviction."

Chapter 37

More Authenticity

Compare their situation with the future ahead of us

We have established the looming overpopulation/limited-resources dilemma. We have surveyed how easy it is becoming for opportunistic religious factions to select, recruit and train members of their flock to do their dirty work. We have examined how this nothing to be lost syndrome can only multiply as the demand/supply graph-lines accelerate apart. It is understood how distressing this bare-facts-of-the-matter picture might be. However, avoiding the issue will only make its inevitable confrontation even more complex than it already is! But how has it been allowed to reach this senseless level? Only now are two immense social issues combining into a survival threatening predicament. The only people who are fully aware of all the terrible implications have neither the courage or the material incentive to declare their awareness of the consequent social upheaval to their supporters. It is a case of letting sleeping dogs lie. Imagine the strength of the pent-up energy when the masses are told about the coming Armageddon! Can you imagine the public's reaction to being told that the only answer is to strictly control parenthood and to limit food, energy and resources?

Worse still is the anticipation of how the cheated and subsequently imperilled populace will react to the revelation and its profusion of spin-off predicaments! There is a large proportion of hungry and angry people who would resort to the rule of the jungle. The strongest and most ruthless will be able to seize and keep whatever might be in short supply. It is e understandable why governments might feel hesitant about revealing the impending horrors to their electorate.

This is uncomfortable, but that doesn't render it any less factual or rational. It might be distressing in that it directly defies everything that most have been brought up to implicitly believe in. This could tempt some to dismiss it rather than t examining its validity. However, some might not have the fortitude or the intellect to scrutinize the carefully-explained opinions that have been offered. We can equate this sort of distress with Charles Darwin's revelations, which directly contradicted contemporary beliefs. Such a situation glaringly illustrates human stubbornness.

However anguished many of the faithful might feel when they finally concede that sacred texts can be factually unreliable, they can take comfort in the knowledge that religion has promoted the establishment of social standards. It might be early days as yet, but the radical cults are gaining strength and momentum with heightening antagonism. World stability is on a horrifying frictionless slope. It is a frightening picture.

I have presented the logical and reasoned-out causes and philosophies behind the origins and growth of the burgeoning dilemma, and how this is being incubated and legitimised by both the Ingredients described in the previous chapter. Coupled with the increasing fragility of the financial conditions as can be seen in our news bulletins, how long will it be before the weakest of those already less-secure nations go to the wall? What will happen to them then? The thin end of a very nasty wedge can be seen in those state bail-outs and even the weakening US economy. The repercussions when one of the larger buttress economies drains the far from inexhaustible loan funds doesn't bear thinking about!

Unless such problems are recognised, intelligently confronted and positively resolved, then the future and our outlook show a grim picture of mass anarchy for us and our offspring. What clear thinking potential parent would wish to bring a child into a world of hunger and hatred, emotions that the ruthless religious activist can so easily exploit.

It is this particular aspect of the mindlessly-ignored crisis which needs to be emphasised. Hopeless and undernourished comfort-seekers desperately crowd into places of worship to find sanctuary from the hostile world, some sympathetic rhetoric and the smallest chink of hope. The matter of forgiveness takes on a more meaningful significance. Any exploitative guru could visualise such a ripe opportunity when he sees it in his congregation. The promise of after-life recompense has a huge potential that can be capitalised upon. In the situation of such obvious and demonstrated wretchedness and hatred, it doesn't take a lot of imagination to see how this potential can be activated and why the church would want it to be!

It is a bleak outlook, but it cannot be denied that the dilemma of our overexploited and overcrowded planet can only deteriorate into anarchy if this blind sleepwalk into disaster is allowed to continue unchecked. This puts the ball right back into our own court. It is we in the developed world who are best positioned financially and psychologically to take the initiative. As we belong to societies that are sufficiently intellectually mature and spiritually realistic to see the strength and extent of the delusions which have caused and continue to endorse these conundrums, then it is only we who have the capacity to set the example and show the way out of the impending disaster. If we just sit back and wait for some sort of divine intervention, then we are quite predictably doomed!

Chapter 38

The Choice of which Path to Follow is Ours

We can only prepare for the coming dilemma if we are aware of its advancing!

Recognition of both the severity of the crisis and the inherent dangers of its being ignored are by far the biggest hurdles. There are some people who just cannot or will not accept that they can ever have been wrong, or that the stories they have heard and implicitly believed might have been unsound, or that any parental guidance could have been based upon out-of-date misinformation, or that any stories in scripture can have been fabricated for whatever reason!

It is an immature response, but it isn't a crime to have been misinformed. It certainly isn't one to admit to having been given wrong information. In any case, evaluating and accepting new and updated information, whether or not it contests previous understandings is, by definition, learning.

Our human reluctance to revise an outlook in the light of new evidence might not be the most intelligent path, but it would be interesting to know what proportion of readers automatically recoiled at the thought of even considering any changes from their traditional beliefs and understandings. All the more credit to those who read-on against this!

However, it is the reader's prerogative to dismiss a thesis in order to protect their instinctive ideals. It is the volume of such entrenched or prejudiced insularity that will probably present the biggest barrier to the confrontation of the issue. It can only be hoped that this barrier will eventually self-destruct under the weight of its own fallibility. In this case, blind stubbornness is a deadly danger!

History shows how fierce religious belligerence has actively impeded the pursuit and revelation of scientific discoveries and the advance of knowledge. History can also be referred to as standing evidence of how society's fickle opinions can change almost overnight!

Segregation was still extant only a few decades ago in the US. When Martin Luther King made his iconic "I have a dream" speech, he was later assassinated! In 2014, Barack Obama is well into his second term and is the living evidence of how such a huge nation can change its long-standing opinions. There will always be discrimination, but the days of blind intransigence can be banished to the shadier and more shameful chapters of history.

Intelligent re-evaluation of long-entrenched doctrines can positively turn around nationwide opinions. If it can happen to colour-prejudice, there's no reason to think that those long-entrenched religious-based beliefs shouldn't be replaced by commonsensical ones in precisely the same way! It is, after all, not only clearly obvious to those who are prepared to see the evidence, but if you think about it in a sensible and open-minded way, it's also a matter of humanity's self-preservation!

There is an obstacle less obvious than stubbornness to be addressed. It also deals with perspective: where we stand in the real cosmos and what an insignificant entity each and every one of us really is. Why should we think that we're anything special, or indeed anything more than just well-advanced animals? This gives us a different frame of reference and broaches the conjecture that our assumptions and beliefs have to be accepted as the truth and never disputed.

The next chapter is an illustrative analogy which is hoped to put a few doubts to rest.

Chapter 39

Imagine…

Another analogy that might help to put things into perspective

Visualise yourself enjoying the ownership of a large, well-established pond. You and your friends are able to enjoy many happy hours there relaxing on the grass banks and watching the many forms of life under the surface of the water. All the different strains of fish, crustaceans, grubs, algae, water plants are busily getting on with their lives. Each one exists within the confinements of its own micro-environment. Without any external source of energy, other than the light and the warmth of the sun, they are all able to flourish and breed. Some might be predatorily dependent on a few of the others, whilst the prey-creatures bring into practise their own, programmed-in methods of awareness and guile to avoid being eaten. Sheer luck plays an important part in the survival/reproduction role that they have been born into. If they survive to die a natural death, their bodies are either consumed as carrion by a scavenger-species or recycled by decomposing into nutrients upon which other life-forms are able to grow, and hence feed back into the never-ending cycle of life.

Life within the bounds of that self-contained environment autonomously re-circulates within its own balance of sustainability. Each separate creature is part of a system that is numerically controlled by food-chain demands and by the physical limits of the environment. They are not aware of anything outside the water's surface and the lake's banks or shoreline. In general, they have no reason or need to look outside their environment or world. There is quite sufficient food and cover for their limited requirements. There might be a few more specialised, though not necessarily more intelligent, creatures that have evolved and become programmed so that when the time is right for their own immediate or subsequent reproduction-cycle purposes, they can naturally and involuntarily metamorphose into a completely different form of air-breathing, water-independent creature. Once on land or in the air, they instinctively adopt their re-patterned existence. Life continues, but in a different way, without them being told or shown how to do it.

All of those life-varieties within and outside the lake's limits, possess neither the need nor the intelligence to work out what exists beyond the limits of their own confines. Some might not even be aware that there is a world beyond which they can see or sense.

However, this water world belongs to you. It's your property and you can do whatever you wish with it. It is within your capacity to do virtually anything that might or might not influence the self-sustaining environment of your lake. Anything from gently rippling the surface of the water so that just a few alarmed entities make a defensive dive for cover, to that of ruthlessly land-filling across the entire area and terminating all of the life that exists within that world.

The power of life, its quality and its termination are in your hands. But none of those innumerable little life forms is aware of that. It is beyond their natural and intellectual capacity to be in any way cognisant of anything outside the confines of their world. As far as all of the lake-life is concerned, you might represent their god.

There are two purposes to this analogy. The first is to illustrate how all those creatures live their own lives and die within the confines that they need to be aware of. Just like most of us, in fact. Some of them have access to or basic perception of a world beyond the boundaries they have evolved to live within, but their perception of any outer-pond space is dictated by their individual and natural life-pattern needs, and also by their very limited mental capacity and visual restrictions. None of them needs to be aware of the earth or space!

Again, like most of us. However, all of this is within the bounds of our continually-expanding sphere of knowledge. We don't know it all any more than those little pond-creatures do! After all, it is only within the last few decades that we have been physically able to explore the space that is, comparatively speaking, right next door to our planet.

A lot more recently, however, we have advanced such that we can acknowledge the fact that the vastness of space is infinite. It is completely indeterminable by us from this minute datum-point we call Earth. We may never be able to do more than hazard an intelligent guess at what, if anything, is beyond the extremity of space that is expanding away from us at the speed of light, simply because of that physical actuality!

Jeffrey Kluger wrote in *Time* magazine in 2011 that we are '...in an observable Universe with a radius of some 14 billion light years.' The speed of light is some 186,000 miles per second, so this is quite a mileage. It is this almost unimaginable expanse of the universe's <u>known</u> vastness that needs to be kept in mind when considering the matter of traditional beliefs.

Just as our water-creatures have specific awareness limits, we have now reached the frontier of our own perceivable spectrum. The pond-species aren't mindful of any existence beyond that which they can see, and nor are we. The only difference is that our species is intelligent enough to <u>know</u> that we don't know. I am far from being a physicist. I have a limited awareness of some of the wonders in the universe, but am only crudely able to visualise the enormity of it all. However, I acknowledge my own intellectual limits and accepting that I don't and never will know all the answers (although many like to think that they do). I refer to those who might feel the need to convince others that it is they who are privileged to have all of the answers and must be believed! We can probably all name a few of them. However, as Socrates said: "Wiser is he who is aware of his ignorance."

The first purpose of the analogy was to liken our creatures' awareness and the size of their environment to ours. Although ours is immeasurably greater in size, we still have our knowledge limitations and also, again no less than our little creatures, don't know all the answers. Unlike our pondlife, we are smart enough to learn. Or, at least, those who don't think that they know it all are...

The second purpose is to put the god-belief into a proper perspective. However anyone likes to picture god, as far as the pondlife is concerned it is you, the magnificent, out-of-reach almighty who has the power of life and death over them and everything else. The only reason you can claim that eminence is because your 'subjects' don't know any better. That also applies to us. However, we are smart enough to learn and are learning by the day.

Chapter 40

Can You See the Similarity?

The purpose and the meaning behind this correlation

The conclusions drawn in the last chapter are worth spending a little more time on. The mysteries of time, life and the aspect of new dimensions might all be resolved for us eventually, but the quest for knowledge must continue if we are to live up to our human perspicacity. That both characterises the human race and made us what we are. It is self-defeating ignominy and arrogance to ostentatiously claim, as so many of us like to do, that we need to look no further. By exercising this belief, we deliberately block out anything which doesn't agree with this conjecture. As a result, we actively obstruct the progress of knowledge. The problem, as might be expected, is that not a lot of people know that. They just listen to and quietly accept as actuality any stories that might emanate from their church's rostrum and take it as the easy way out

It is common sense to relegate all of those beliefs in enigma-answering myths and fables to no more than the historical records of how we developed from the social aspect. If we can look to the future rather than the past it can only further our intellectual advancement. Our past has all played a valuable part in our development but must not hinder our progress any longer. In order for us to open our minds to progress, we must close our minds to the traditions that have played their part in our past, but have now run their course and welcome new learning without anxiety that it challenges old learning.

Just like our little pond-creatures, the fact that the outside existence isn't known about doesn't mean that it doesn't exist. However, human beings are so inordinately presumptuous that we think that we know all the answers. If we cannot find a convenient one, then we make up one that will fit the bill.

Historically, and in the absence of real facts, we had sufficient intelligence and dialogue to think up and broadcast any plausible tale to provide much-demanded answers without any fear of correction. That was what people wanted, so they happily took it aboard. From that point onwards, the conveniently-indisputable story was used as an answer to virtually every conceivable question, strengthening and growing progressively less contestable with the passage of time. There were many instances of the same strategy all around the world, hence the variations in detail, but it is obvious how imprinting evolved in this way?

It is a human trait to resolve a conundrum by contriving an answer to soothe our threatened self-esteem. If it's an answer which provides a congenial and comforting theory that satisfies all of the questions what could be better? This logical sequence makes the argument perfectly viable and certainly not sacrilegious. In fact, this argument is no less respectful than the lessons at school which taught us how to collect, assess and present facts as they appear.

Chapter 41

Every Perspective has its Vanishing-Point

Rounding-off a few rough edges

The pondlife analogy illustrated knowledge's limitations as a result of several inherent factors. These included the new information's credibility in the light of accredited facts, and the researcher's mental capacity or willingness to change an existing understanding to a new one.

As far as the pond-creatures are concerned, there are other limitations. These are the boundaries affected by the pond's extremities and pondlife's actual need for further knowledge. Although a few specimens might have been able to metamorphose and leave the water later in their lives, it is unlikely that they knew of this beforehand, as their brains had neither the capacity nor the incentive to speculate on what exists outside this natural boundary.

However, just suppose for a moment that one branch of a species were to mutate such that they somehow obtained this capability. Imagine that they were able to congregate together, to look up at the green banks and the rippling water surface which so positively limited their insight and perception. Then, just as we did so long ago, they would ask themselves the obvious question about life beyond.

Importantly, as we did (and do!), they would soon make their own presumptions and hypotheses which would provide satisfying answers about their existence. They might also ask what happens when they die. That out-of-reach realm provides a convenient answer to that question too.

Had they the power, these creatures' ancestors might have told them anything from the dredging-out of great swathes of life-supporting reed-beds, to the incursion of poisonous pollutants like crop-sprays that had found their way into their 'atmosphere' with terrible results! But whatever the scale of the unforeseen devastation, from the creatures' point of view it would have been what our insurers would call "An act of God," meaning something that can neither be predicted nor avoided. How would they account for such forces? What would be the only fulfilling and conveniently-remote reason that could explain it all? They would have come to the only possible conclusion that would fit in with their presumptions and hypotheses: a god-figure.

To expand along that line of thinking, the visualised god-figure would also provide a focus for gratitude. It would serve as a controlling force which might punish or reward. Worship and prayer to augment this belief would soon establish itself.

This is imaginary, but it illustrates a comparison which might help to put evolutionary psychology into a different frame of reference and aid the favourable reception of its otherwise disturbing hypotheses. The only hurdle which might constrain full acceptance of the god-origin theory would be the comparison of the parallels between the limitations of the pond-creatures' perceptive bounds and ours. Ours might be wider, but they are vastly more limited than many like to think. They are limits, nevertheless, which means that beyond these frontiers is the vastness of the unknown. And that's just on the physical register! All told, we're pretty ignorant, but not a lot of people know that.

To summarise this analogy we, just like our little water-entities, are unaware about so much. The more that we discover, the more we realise how little we know!

As far as our pond-life is concerned, all the unmanageable 'devastations' or 'inconveniences' of their daily life would be shrugged off as being from "out there" or as being unpreventable by foresight. So how would they account for these influences and forces? What would be the only fulfilling and conveniently-remote answer to it all? What else other than that which has been described above, and presented (in our imaginary world) as an inevitability?

These mutations wouldn't be aware of their intelligence limits, but we are in a different situation. Our powers of reasoning diverge along one of two paths. The first is where the unknown" is kept in check by belief. The bigger the unknown, then greater the strength of the pressures applied to enforce such belief. Many will be conscious of the exacting demands that are made by some faiths, where all of the 'unanswerables' have a simple and incontestable solution. (The "Cosythink Culture" in action?). The second of these two categories is where belief is either put aside or subjectively investigated and maybe disputed. If the wiser person is he who is aware that he doesn't know, then the two categories quite naturally fall into place. The entire purpose of including this analogy is so that the logic that endorses it might make its contemplation a little easier, and its possible acceptance less disquieting.

It might also put another aspect of religious ritual into a new perspective. It presents a numerically-judicious and more realistic frame of reference to a much-practised (albeit little-reciprocated) ritual or personal invocation: prayer. There are over seven thousand million souls on Earth. Who is going to fit in all those pleas for Auntie Mary, for a better life for everyone, or for a pet dog's bad leg? If there were any evidence of prayer working outside coincidence, it might be a different matter. I have yet to see any proof of prayer working, although I do know about the placebo effect!

Without denying the existence of God or gods, I want to constructively present a rationalised outlook on unrationalised traditions. What I promote is the opening-up of the investigative discipline that blind belief prohibits. After all, any new investigation might very well reveal proper and undeniable evidence of the actual existence of God, rather than having to trust mere fiction. I think that anyone would agree with this.

There are some believers who like to put forward the start of life on Earth as being positive proof of the existence of God.

However it might have been that life on Earth actually (and the amino-acid and proton gradient theories are making some interesting progress at this time), but as yet, we simply do not know! That lack of knowledge includes the religious account. If we preclude seeking the answer because we think that we've already got it, then we'll never be able to find out if we were wrong!

The title of this book is significant: There's None so Blind as He Who *will* Not See.

The emphasised unwillingness to see is probably abundantly clear by now. It might have registered with the observant reader quite early in the book how frustratingly bewildering I find the almost complete and abject denials of such grim situations. The deeper I looked into the conundrums, the more incomprehensible it appeared to me how something world-threatening can be so casually ignored! It is like walking towards a cliff-top that you know is there, but with eyes tightly shut to avoid seeing what you don't want to see! Inane!

When I introduced some of the topics in this book in conversation, some of the responses I received were almost unbelievable in their self-interest and thoughtlessness. I mentioned the emotive subjects of uncontrolled reproduction and religious intransigence to test the water. Interestingly, it was the suggested need for restricting procreation that seemed to raise instant and almost hostile antagonism. When the subject was even casually mentioned to both males and females, it very often released a barrage of arguably-illogical platitudes. I heard such hackneyed and overworked phrases as "it's my human right to have kids", "Without children no family can be complete" and "We need to have children to bond our marriage properly." All of these responses are grand-sounding but meaningless. But, whatever the motivation, these stock phrases with their instant, passionate intensity, exemplify and illustrate just how deeply-ingrained instinctive programming can be. It is of equal relevance in this context how spontaneously and impulsively any such misgivings about the confrontation and management of that culture are repulsed.

For those who have been able to see and appreciate the multi-faceted magnitude of the dilemma it is a frightening demonstration of the hurdle's size. It's almost a clear-cut case of simple and obvious logic versus a strong compulsion that emanates from an inbuilt but unconscious instinct.! Perhaps it is simply the acting out of subliminal, ritualised procedures. Nobody likes to admit to having been 'programmed' into anything, and nobody is willing to concede that, by taking appropriate precautions, there need be a problem in the first place! If we accept a solution, we take on a lot of trouble. Who wants to admit that? As Bob Dylan so beautifully and eloquently phrased in his song "Blowin' In The Wind" (Columbia Records N.Y., Released August 1963). "Yes, and how many times can a man turn away, pretending that he doesn't see? The answer, my friend, is blowin' in the wind..." However, the longer that it's left "blowin' in the wind", the more grim and distressing it will ultimately be to find and inaugurate a humanitarian solution. Although this could be a counter-productive comment, it might well be that we are already past the point of no return. Perhaps a benign answer even now is not achievable.

The entire purpose of this book is to identify, analyse and objectively present the imminent and forecast problems, the result of their examination or evaluation and their projected potential outcomes. It does not presume to provide or even suggest an answer to them. Recognition is the first step.

To "...turn away pretending that he doesn't see?" would be the response of naïve individuals who seem to be unable to comprehend that problems of the magnitude and depth of those that have been illustrated here do not just go away. We can see for ourselves and acknowledge the evidence all around the world: the poverty, the financial breakdowns, the Middle East's and Africa's crumbling stability, our own austerity measures and the slow but inexorable increase in the cost of living. All these are symptoms of a sickening world. If they are not attended to, the patient will die. Basic evolution is evidence how nature regulates numbers by the principles of unsustainability. But waiting for a natural holocaust to happen is sheer stupidity.

It certainly takes a discerning and very understanding person to concede that they have been misinformed about religion. However, nobody is above being misinformed, and there is clearly no shame or dishonour in changing one's mind over issues which have been corrected by science, geology, and plain common sense. One is all the more praiseworthy when openly admitting to have been wrong, not to mention better-educated. Like it or not, "The times, they are a-changin'!"

Chapter 42

Looking Back in a Different Light

A summary

This book has been compiled in full knowledge that a large proportion of its contents will probably be more than just disturbing to the average reader. This is due to the way it openly challenges blind and unthinking compliance to the natural procreativity instincts, and also because it offers contentions that clearly and logically dispute the validity of both the bases and the perpetuation of religious principles.

I hope that even the most religious or socially complacent person would have been honest and objective enough to read and perceptively weigh up all my observations. I have written on population/government concealments and their clandestine aims; the growing top-heaviness of the world's demand/production balance; the surmised religious bases with their natural psychological channelling and sequences, growth and crystallisation of religious beliefs and their diversities through the many ages; and the frightening extent and sheer inevitability of the truly horrific conclusions which have been rationalised and put forward. All of these are the direct result of our mindless and dogged failure to accept and confront these issues earlier.

The magnitude of both the approaching crisis and the inherent stubbornness of those who refuse to change their traditional outlook demanded very careful presentation. A delicate balance had to be achieved and I hope that both the sceptical traditionalists and those who might be becoming aware have both been served.

I don't know when the world's populace will finally become aware of the impending crisis. The "blindness" factor has a ridiculously strong hold on so many people. They would rather pretend that facts don't exist than accept and face them be-cause they are uncomfortable to concede. That is the level of mentality that not only is the cause of this conundrum, but that will take the relatable reality of a disaster or two before the majority finally falls in! Catastrophes like those that will blow up in the Middle-East soon, like the coming bankruptcy of debt-ridden states, the civil wars and famines in Africa, the festering nuclear fragility in the Middle East and North Korea, the African and South American economies that are based on corruption and drugs and so on, whilst nearer home there's the increasing fuel, energy and living costs, the (real) increasing numbers of unemployed and benefit-dependent people who have to be supported and, after all that, the recognition that this is all going to get worse. We're on a frictionless slope to the inevitable!

But it will take one or two of these or other disasters to occur before it will really hit the fan. When the masses realise the size and imminence of the problem and when the future (or absence of it) becomes self-evident, when the starvation and (for the traditionalists) non-existence of heavenly help makes the disaster an inevitability, <u>then</u> anarchy will become a reality. When people realise their own lives are on the line, the law of the jungle will take over!

It is when the penny finally drops that the contents of this book will become relevant and understood by the unenlightened or dubious.

This book is trying to put into perspective the size and the imminence of the ticking time-bomb that we are complacently sitting upon, and while we persist in pretending that it's not really there, then there's no hope of its ever being defused.

To close, my convictions about the coming Armageddon are absolute. The evidence is there. But there are many who might need more than just a little prompting. They might not be fully convinced that the observations and the conclusions drawn and offered cannot be true because it's all so macabre and shocking. The fact that something is hideous unimaginably horrifying is certainly no reason that it cannot materialise. Just have a look at a few of the statistics about the last world war: the numbers that were deliberately murdered as well as the fighting and civilian fatalities and casualties. Have a subjective look at the politics that led up to the wars and ask yourself, "with all the evidence that was there to be seen, why didn't we recognise the symptoms for what they were and then we could have prevented it". Just as it says in the book…

Aware eyes see things a lot more realistically than uninformed eyes do.

By way of a post-script, I have reproduced an anonymous cartoon I saw on a noticeboard a few years ago, as accurately as best can be remembered. It is offered as a light-hearted finale in the hope that it will help to illustrate and show the ethics of religious introduction and beliefs in a fresh light.

YOU'LL NOT BELIEVE THIS! TEN MINUTES AGO I DIDN'T KNOW WHAT A CHRISTIAN IS, AND NOW I ARE ONE!
NLY 10 US

Question: What do you call long-standing beliefs that have no form of corroboration for their authenticity, many of which are openly conceded to be based on "visions" (hallucinations), some of which are physical impossibilities and others that are even submitted to be no more than one man's account, and all of these improbabilities not only being sourced up to several millennia in the past, with only the word-of-mouth transmission for sometimes many decades before actually being recorded, but also very significantly being passed onto each progressive generation through formative-year indoctrination, (the parental "It's a fact because I KNOW that it is!"…….)?

Answer: (Clue; where dogma stifles logic.) "Tradition".

Question: What do you call the act of maturing-out of the credulous acceptance-without-evidence syndrome; where (the parentally-advised) belief in one's "knowing" the answers actually prohibits all prospect of any propitious or potentially educational lines of thought that could completely alter one's theological outlook; where the ritual of regular worship and prayer (however unresponded-to!) is gradually changing from a straightforward 'thanking' rite to one of 'insurance' ("just in case there's something in it"); where the evidence of growing incredibility and the decreasing authenticity of the readings and sermons steadily bely and erode the entire principle of "faith"; and where it can be seen that the majority of world conflicts (as well as that of the fast- approaching social breakdown when world population exceeds that which the Earth can support and which, see text, regimes can no longer conceal and avoid) are directly or indirectly initiated by (or for the benefit of) one belief or another (the 'excuses' "Holy War" and "Ethnic Cleansing" might sound familiar?) So, what is this breakout from traditional, religiously-enforced blindness called?

Answer: "Evolution", "Progress", "Movement Onwards", "Advancement", "Natural Development", "Basic Intelligence", "Self-improvement", even "Common Sense".....

Question: What do you call those who indiscriminately "pump" more and more souls onto an Earth that is visibly fast running-out of the resources needed to support them?

Answer: (a) They all, if you think about it, are the "None so Blind" referred-to, but (b) in the case of those with the intelligence to foresee the cataclysm: They are actually guilty of being party to the approaching holocaust by exacerbating the situation <u>in full awareness</u> of what's at stake "...pretending that he cannot see". A case of passing the buck onto the next generation in hope that (and how selfish is this?) it comes to a head in their lifetime, not ours! Just how "Blind" can one pretend to be? The answer, in the case of those without the insight: Pitiable victims of circumstance.

So, will this be The End?

The Real Facts of Life

1) **Personal Concern.**
   These verses are submitted, whilst aware some won't agree
   With views and thoughts put forward to assess,
   But changing situations in a world of apathy
   Demands we <u>see</u> the plight we must address.

2) **The History.**
   In times long past the need to fortify our kind endured
   As life itself was tenuous and short.
   Our Earth held vast resources then. Available, assured,
   Whilst in its vastness man's effect was nought.

3) **The Reasoning.**
   The dictate of such circumstances made, and set, the code
   On which our social structures formed their base.
   But now? Our stretched resources and increasing overload
   Demand we recognise what we must face.

4) **Deliberations about the Inevitable.**
   To not mince words, we must now face that boundaries have been met
   Where food and oil and water from our Earth
   No longer are sustainable. It's MORE than just a threat!
   Resources less than needs? Then limit birth!

5) **Overpopulation, the Emerging Calamity.**
   Discomfiting it might be, not everybody's taste
   But light amusement's not this poem's aim.....
   When facts are indisputable but simply are not faced,
   We must ensure concealment's not to blame.

6) **Consider, for Example.....**
   The "Third World". Racked by famine and by poverty as shown
   In news reports. Whilst (blind and overfed),
   We need weigh-up those wretches who, through no fault of their own,
   Find themselves without a home or bread.

7) **There's None so Blind....**
Compassionate viewers shed a tear, then "Switch that telly off!"
Saddened, yes, but correlated, no.
Why can't they see its global and we're in that self-same trough,
It's coming, and there isn't long to go!

8) **.....as He Who WILL Not See.**
Endured by those unfortunates, and here (to less extent),
Those destitute and homeless on the road
Are live omens of what's to come; of OUR predicament
When matters 'come to head' as facts forebode.

9) **The "Facts"?**
With populations multiplying faster all the time,
Resources drying-up to make this grave,
This situation's unsustainability is prime.
The Human Race: THAT'S what we have to save!

10) **The Choice is Ours (that's if there's still any choice about it!).**
So what (if not blind ignorance), and who (if not perverse),
Would sanctify this self-destructive course?
"Survival-breeding" is long-gone; it's now exact reverse.
Perhaps our breeding cart's before the horse?

11) **Let's Start with the Inevitable Unemployment Problem.**
One must admit, if honest, and with work's becoming scarce
(Technology's reducing even more),
That unemployment must increase; we have to acquiesce
This simple, clear and certain basic law!

12) **Weighing-up the Facts of the Matter.**
More people, then, with less to share.....the future's grim indeed,
If logic and good sense are cast aside.
The future's clear, wise couples see, whilst "disregarders" feed
The growing problem! Can that be denied?

13) **Basic Essentials versus Primitive Instincts.**
    At risk of causing disaccord, one stands against the flow
    Of customary rituals and scenes.
    As sometimes-less-than-solvent couples keep that status quo
    By bearing more to share their meagre means. BBBB

14) **As so Often Happens.....**
    As passions rise so caution dies, engulfed in new-love's fire,
    Then waning-afterglow precedes unease
    That kindles in the light of dawn. And, yes, one might enquire
    How many "Planned" are really "C'est la vie"s?

15) **And what about all of those Unthinking Rituals?**
    "Congratulations" and "Well done" (predictably) friends say
    Aware that, with their means and freedom lost,
    An honest "So, you've made your bed, and in it you must lay!"
    Might open naïve eyes, however 'glossed'.

16) **To Elucidate on the Theme,**
    "Congratulations" signals praise. Its aim? To recognise
    Respect for an achievement fought and won!
    So what (if not sheer lack of thought) promotes its thin disguise
    When dignifying careless, costly fun?

17) **Furthermore.....**
    "Congratulations", surely should (expressed in honesty)
    Be kept for prudent couples taking care;
    Enjoying all the fruits of love whilst leaving themselves free
    To live their lives "An unencumbered pair".

18) **Hence.**
    No worries, ties, restraints or tasks; unburdened, free to do
    Whatever whims or fancies they decide.
    The benefits are countless when "Two incomes funding two"
    Instead of "One funds three" can't be denied!

19) **Oh, and don't forget about this.**
    Long nights awake, the mess, the cries, the fragile tempers frayed.....
    Maternal instinct clouds the parent's eye,
    Traditionally veiling any traumas then relayed

To routine ears that crowd to glorify.

20) As well as.....
Sheer agony in giving birth; incessant, loud appeals,
Those unplanned, noisy torments seem to be
Unending in their petulance; compulsory ordeals....
Those days of blissful peace? A memory!

21) …..all the Obligations.
And these appeals <u>must</u> be addressed, no matter when or where
Or knowing whether genuine of feigned
For, as a child begins to talk, it also comes aware
A "Raucous squawk" means warmth and goodies gained.

22) (You <u>must</u> have heard them in the Supermarket?). But remember....
It's at this point one might recall the caution at the start
That what is being said might cause unease.
But is this not a case where facts we're 'trained' not to impart
<u>Need</u> be aired, so everybody sees?

23) To Continue.
So, on the rituals proceed, as "Little monkey!" learns
To supplement a deftness learnt by test;
And, reaching teens, deceit might be another of concerns
The loving parents fear, but daren't suggest.

24) Nobody, not even One's Own Child, is Perfect.
Whilst smoking, drug-addiction, drink and other vices loom
Alongside other worries such as school-
Attendance and examinations, homework, hours of gloom,
Foul language and the yearn to ridicule.....

25) The Easy Way Out?
Detachment doesn't solve it; give an inch, they take a yard
And fam'ly-life becomes a trial of wills.
Most parents will deny this fact! It's easier to regard
Acceptance as "The lesser of two ills".

26) So, the Carrot.....?
Predictably, the tale evolves with worries, stress and fears
Of things like AIDS, corruption, dope and lies',
Whilst faithful, loving parents try imploring, shedding tears,

Indulging, listening, trying to compromise.

27) ….. or The Stick?
'Til one or other sees the light, perceives the base abuse,
With one of three alternative results.
The first, with luck, when Mum and Dad as partners introduce
Restraints and ethics as befit adults.

28) But Firmness is Essential.
Complied-with when unerringly applied without disdain,
Such "House Rules!" set the limit all agree.
The family can reconnect the links within its chain.
Respect and love results in harmony.

29) Or This Might Happen.
The second of the three 'results' when sympathetic friends,
Voice "Freedom!", "Do what <u>you</u> want!", "Life's your own!"
Persuade the ruffled rebel that the world out there extends
A welcoming enticement for the lone.

30) And the Result?
So, from the "Boring!" family fold, the dissident withdraws
To face alone the grasping world outside…..
From there, it's circumstantial, but may very well have cause
To recognise the comforts been decried.

31) And the 'Worst Case Scenario'?
The third and cruellest consequence develops as result
Of one or other parents taking side
In actively supporting scornful youth against adult!
And splitting any marriage open wide…..

32) Enough Said. Takes a Deep Breath.
Of course, it mightn't be like this. But how can one be sure,
As juveniles will meet a mix of souls?
It's also just a chance of fate how youngsters might mature
For parenthood has limited controls.

33) Rose-tinted Glasses?
"MY child would never be like that! He's cherished, fed and well….."
Of course, all parents rush to remonstrate.
But, think about it sensibly, no one on Earth can tell
How <u>any</u> life is influenced by fate!

34) **Remember?**
Parental care's inconsequential; just one word or wink
Can tempt the very best-raised teenage ears.
Of course one hopes one's child will be a paragon, but think,
Be mindful of your own ingenuous years!

35) **Let's Look at the Situation a Little Less Personally.**
<u>The Unemployed.</u> These numbers swell as high-tech methods make
Less work to do, and that one can't deny.
But people without jobs must be maintained, make no mistake,
So those who <u>have</u> jobs must finance supply.

36) **And bring Realism into the Equation.**
"Governmental Estimates" for numbers unemployed
Intentionally axe the true amount.
It doesn't take a lot of wit to see how they avoid
Advising their electorate <u>how</u> they count.

37) **Unprincipled? Or just Self-preservation?**
How many heads, one has to ask, would show above the hide
If all the part-time jobs were reassessed,
Returned to full-time employees to easily provide
An equal output? Three-to-one at best?

38) **Then there's the Academic Scam!**
And that's just one big method used to cut the jobless sum!
School-leavers gladly contribute the same
With "Excellent" they all, it seems, as every single one
Pass their exams, and "Uni." is the game.

39) **Another Part of the Governmental Cover-up.**
So, several years as students, not counting "Gap-year" perks
To gain "Degrees" of often trifling use,
Means many, many person-years (and this is how it works),
Not claiming; hence the "Unemployed's reduce.

40) **And That's not All.....**
And then, of course, the lecturers and all supporting staff,
Providing and sustaining as they do.....
There'd many <u>less</u> be necessary, maybe less than half
If only <u>worthwhile</u> applicants went through!

41) …..the Concealment Ploys.
    The Unemployed, Part-timers, most Students wasting years,
    The easy "Work-excused", the "Cash-in-hand"....
    When <u>properly</u> accounted-for then (not as it appears)
    We're 'Underjobbed' and badly 'Overmanned'.

42) **And that's Just Locally; but it's a World-Wide Problem!**
    Resources, worldwide, dwindle from the mushrooming demand,
    Exhausted land no longer yields the grain;
    Our oil and coal are running-out; the forests levelled and
    Denuded soil erodes from wind and rain.

43) <u>A Must-See;</u> **"When the Rivers Run Dry" by Fred Pearce.....**
    Essential need of water, that most assume's on tap,
    Is one more peril eas'ly passed aside;
    But rivers dammed and rash abuse soon mutilates the map....
    In saline dustbowls, no-one can reside!

44) **As Water-tables Drop Away.**
    The climate-change predicament might cause what one observes
    With floods, and storms, and suchlike tragedies,
    But these are merely symptoms as we milk dry our reserves.
    The symptoms source? A TERMINAL disease!

45) **And There's another Hidden Symptom.**
    Unknown to most, but none-the-less profound to many who
    Inhabit lands sustained by water gained
    From aquifers beneath their feet. They're running dry. It's true
    That, global-wide, these lakes are being drained.

46) **Let's Stand Back and Anticipate a Little (while we still can).** Dry, dusty winds across parched plains foretell <u>(for those who'll see)</u>
    This suicidal dead-end that's ahead.
    Our larder's fast becoming bare! Accept this infamy
    And then concede the new road we must tread.

47) **Another View of the Status Quo, but in a New Light?**
    In respect for every parent, and defence for what's been said,

It's true this dark prediction mightn't be;
Alarm, though, is so necessary; seeds of doubt are fed
To open eyes, in order they can see!

48) **But the Ball's in <u>Our</u> Court.**
Rashly-blind dismissal would dangerously stall
Unmasking of this holocaust's advance.
Whilst mass-producing multitudes don't have the wherewithall
For birth-control, we DO! That's circumstance....

49) **"Consciousness" by Rita Carter, Covers this Superbly.**
Thoughtlessly submitting to the fundamental urge;
The starry-eyed "Another's on its way!"
Such programmed-in conformity, unquestioned, unreserved,
Must illustrate that urge the lax obey?

50) **Being Aware of these Issues, though, we <u>can</u> Revise our Views.**
But, there again, it needs a brain to think and plan ahead,
To view, then weigh-up, all that's gained and lost,
To <u>recognise</u> the presence of an instinct that's inbred,
To estimate the <u>full</u> parental cost.

51) **"Instinct that's Inbred"? This is How it Works.**
"Maternal Instinct" (like a faith?), unchallengeably chaste,
Is stated as "A cause above dissent".
One dares not question ethics, or if logic's been misplaced
As "Motherhood's a Gift That's Heaven-sent".....!

52) **And then, Out Comes all the Predictable Rhetoric.....**
"We <u>want</u> a child", or "Kids are what we <u>need</u> to be complete",
And other well-worn clichés blandly reel
From lips of those absolving what is often indiscrete
Carelessness they'd rather not reveal?

53) **And then there's the Biggest Scam of All.**
Let's not forget the guilty faiths that selfishly <u>instruct</u>
Their devotees that "Birth-control's a SIN!"
Religiously, their coffers swell with tythes, donations plucked
From all their naïve followers within!

54) **Ecumenical or just Exploitative?**

Sanctimonious, the claims, that contributions made
(However hard for he who contributes)
Are dues indebted (bounds, in fact) to graciously be paid
For "Gift of Life" and such vague attributes.

55) **Big Business, perhaps?**
Meanwhile, as hoarding "Holy" vaults distend from conquests' loot
These syndicates secure their income's fate,
So, quite aware that more believers means more contribute
Then "Family-Planning's something they must hate!

56) **Like Some T.V. Adverts, Exploiting the Gullible?**
One might well ask, "How spiritual, that takes without remorse
The 'Holy' yields whose assets spawn with time"?
They claim it's "In the name of God", impeccable the cause.....
No wonder birth-control is deemed a crime!

57) **But, if we Stand Back and Apply our Common Sense....**
"Unspiritual", one might have said, "More births we must support",
Or maybe "It's our role, our duty here!"
But ask yourself sincerely, and not without long thought,
<u>Who</u> says we must? <u>We</u> choose the course we steer!

58) **….. and Look at the Future**.
So, <u>is</u> it kind, or spiritual then, to cram more people in
A world already-crowded, growing worse?
Just look ahead a few more years, <u>then</u> say it's not a sin;
Observe what mindless lemmings won't reverse!

59) **And, Not to Mince Words,**
Less work to share, more mouths to feed; and so the spirals bite,
Those certainties we cannot disregard.
That cliché "Gift of Birth" is dead, to put the context right
A child "is hoist by someone else's petard".

60) **Confronting that Which Might have Been Evaded. Now?**
It must be clear to anyone with realistic sense
That procreation's not a trivial thing.

In bringing-up a family, the "Seen" plus "Veiled" expense,
When viewed aside congestion, bears a sting.

61) **To Reiterate**.
As said before, we <u>have</u> the choice, so foolish we must be
To take on what we needn't, <u>with its price!</u>
A cat, or dog, (or hamster, yet!) provides the company
With no environmental sacrifice.

62) **And, just to Remind Again**.....
When once a couple's procreation "programming" has sprung,
Restrictions tie their plans and hoped-for schemes,
For parenthood revolves around the welfare of their young.
Their bubble's burst. And, with it, freedom's dreams.

63) **.....with the BIG, Personal Advantages there to be Gained**.....
With 'pills' or hysterectomy, insurance is secure
For she enjoying 'intimate delights';
Whilst painless, quick vasectomy protects a man for sure
From 'blunders' in those "Nothing special" nights.....

64) **Disadvantages? None. Benefits? Countless**.
So simple and so obvious; and assets so profuse!
That some just blindly spurn it is absurd.
Sterility will guarantee that "Parenthood's" misuse
Is inconceivable (to coin a word).

65) **Closing Thoughts**.
Concluding this submission and conceding it disturbs
Complacency unquestioned for so long,
How <u>can</u> these contents be dismissed if, doubts aroused, it curbs
Yet more <u>foredoomed</u> assemblage to the throng?

66) **But, Hopefully, Not Terminally so?**
For thought, consideration, then weighing-up the facts,
This humble verse is planned to instigate.
We all have brains! Let's use them so that unplanned, thoughtless acts
Can be addressed! Just hope we're not too late......

Appendix

Aware it's controversial and response one could expect
From those to whom this article applies,
Impressions were invited (as one's aims are circumspect
And to prejudice one's readers isn't wise!).
It caused no small bewilderment when, as if from script,
Some readers voiced the narrow-minded view.....
"If everybody did it, there'd be no-one left!" they quipped
As if world-wide compliance would ensue.
And what, then, would be simpler than to stop it or reverse
If such an absurd outcome <u>should</u> unfold?
So, if that's the best objection to be set against this verse
Can we <u>afford</u> to leave this, uncontrolled?

Original: July 1991 ("Super poem...." – David Bellamy).
Revisions: January 1992
February 2010
February 2012
February 2013

Jack Levy.